Penguin Education

Success with English   The Penguin Course

General Editor

Geoffrey Broughton,
Lecturer in English as a Foreign Language,
Institute of Education, University of London

Collaborating Committee

J. A. Barnett,
Director of Studies,
Regional Institute of English,
Bangalore

Thomas Greenwood,
Principal, Oxford Academy of English

John Parry,
previously with Schools Television,
British Broadcasting Corporation

Success with English   The Penguin Course

Coursebook 2

Geoffrey Broughton

Illustrations by Quentin Blake

Penguin Books

Penguin Books Ltd, Harmondsworth, Middlesex, England
Penguin Books Inc., 7110 Ambassador Road, Baltimore, Md 21207, U.S.A.
Penguin Books Australia Ltd, Ringwood, Victoria, Australia

First published 1969
Reprinted 1970, 1971 (twice)
Copyright © Geoffrey Broughton, 1969

Filmset in Monophoto Baskerville
by Oliver Burridge Filmsetting Ltd, Crawley
Printed by Times Printers SDN. BHD. Singapore

Unit 1

Exercise 1

What is happening in these pictures?
Ask: What is — doing? e.g. What is the old man doing?
Answer: — is — . e.g. He is talking. *or* He is holding a stick.

to stand, to sit, to hold, to buy, to sell, to put, to look, to write, to ask, to wear.

to sit, to stand, to talk to, to listen to, to go, to wait, to laugh, to read, to carry, to drop.

Exercise 2

Look at the pictures again.

Ask: What was — doing in the	post office	on May 9th? at three o'clock?
	library	on November 24th? at ten minutes to six?

Then answer your questions.

Exercise 3

The people in the pictures are thinking. Say who is thinking each of these sentences.

The old man always buys his stamps from me.
That assistant always makes me wait.
I always phone my wife at three o'clock.
He says the silliest things.
Every week I take my books back to the children's librarian.
I always put my money safely in my handbag.
My mother wants a stamp for this letter.
This man writes the most wonderful books.
I like her because she doesn't laugh at my stick.
Has she got a boy-friend?

1

1

2

1

Exercise 4

Put these broken sentences together correctly, when you have looked at the two pictures again.

Putting her money in her handbag	he dropped his glasses.
Waiting for the assistant to turn round,	
	he wrote down what she said.
Holding up the letter,	she saw the children's library notice.
Talking to his wife on the telephone,	
	she laughed at what he said.
Sitting under the clock,	he talked to the pretty girl.
Looking down in front of the counter,	
	she sold the old man some stamps.
Walking past the book shelves,	she went away from the counter.
Shutting her eyes,	he asked for a stamp.
Holding the flowers behind his back,	
	she began to read a book.
Sitting at the post office counter,	he saw a little boy.

Exercise 5

Make ten true sentences:

In the	post office public library	there's	a woman a man a boy a girl	holding a handbag. selling stamps. talking on the telephone. standing at the counter. holding a letter. holding a book. holding some flowers.

8

1

Now make ten true sentences.

The	woman man boy girl	standing at the counter selling stamps holding a book	in the	post office library

is	small. old. angry. happy. talking. laughing.

Exercise 6

Who says this?

I have brought you some flowers.
I haven't read this book before.
Has she heard me?
That woman has gone now, so I can talk to you.
Have you got the right money, my boy?
Look, I've just bought a new stick.
What have I done with my glasses?
There, I've put it away safely.
What have you got behind your back?
He has always been my favourite writer.

1

Martin's shower

The other day Martin was sitting comfortably in his favourite chair, smoking his pipe. Suddenly he jumped up.

"I'm forgetting the time," he said to himself. "I'm meeting Jillian in half an hour and I haven't had my bath yet. I shall be late."

He ran upstairs two at a time, taking off his clothes as he went, but still smoking his pipe. In the bathroom he stopped to think.

"A shower will be quicker than a bath," he told himself, so he stood in the bath under the shower, and turned the taps on. But he suddenly found that he was still smoking his pipe.

"I must be careful," he thought, "or it will get wet. And I mustn't get my hair wet, or it will take too long to dry it." So he stood under the shower, holding his head to one side.

But it is difficult to have a shower and smoke a pipe and hold your head out of the water, all at the same time. So, beginning to feel angry, Martin turned the shower taps off.

"Perhaps a bath will be quicker. Then I can smoke my pipe and I shan't get my hair wet," he thought. So he turned both the bath taps on, sat down in the warm water and began to wash. For a few minutes he sat there comfortably, washing and smoking, and thinking he was very clever to smoke in the bath. Then suddenly the shower over his head made a little noise and sent a few last drops of water down onto Martin's hair. He threw up his hands and knocked the pipe out of his mouth into the bath water.

Now there were dirty little black bits of tobacco swimming round him in the water. Angrily he jumped out of the bath, pulled out the plug and tried to clean the bath a little as the water went down. Then he was ready to dry himself. But when he looked at himself he found more little bits of tobacco on his face and arms

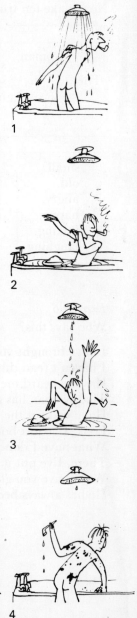

1

2

3

4

and his body. Now his hair was wet, his pipe was wet and he was dirtier than when he first went into the bathroom. Slowly he got into the bath again, and holding his wet pipe in his mouth started to have a shower.

5

Later, when Martin met Jillian he explained why he was late. "I had a shower because I wanted to be quick," he said. "Then I had a bath so that I could smoke my pipe. But when I finished my bath I had all these bits of tobacco on me. So I had another shower."

Jillian laughed. "And your hair's still wet, isn't it?" she said. "You know, when I have a shower, I wear a plastic bath hat. Shall I buy you one?"

"Yes please," Martin said. "Get two. A big one for me and a little one for my pipe."

New words

to smoke, a pipe, to jump, yet, a shower, to turn on/off, a tap, to dry, a noise, a drop, onto, a bit, tobacco, angrily, a bath plug, a body, so that, another.

Exercise 7

Look at the five pictures in the story. Make three sentences for each picture. Like this: Martin is having a shower.
Use "–ing" in each sentence.
Now say your sentences again to somebody, but this time make them questions. Like this: Martin is having a shower, isn't he?

Exercise 8

Now, looking at the same pictures, answer these questions. Give full answers, using "because".

Picture 1
Why did Martin have a shower?
Why did he hold his head to one side?

Picture 2
Why did he have a bath?
Why did he think he was clever?

Picture 3
Why did he throw up his hands?
Why did his pipe fall into the water?

Picture 4
Why did he jump out of the bath?
Why did he try to clean it?

Picture 5
Why did he get into the bath slowly?
Why did he start to have a shower again?

Exercise 9
Make eight true sentences.

Martin had a shower	
He held his head to one side	
He had a bath	
He turned the bath taps on	
He jumped out of the bath	so that
He had a second shower	
Jillian always wears a bath hat	
Martin wants a little plastic hat	

he could have a bath.
he could be early to meet Jillian.
he could clean it.
he could wash the bits off himself.
he didn't get his hair and his pipe wet.
he could still smoke his pipe.
he can smoke his pipe in the bath.
she doesn't get her hair wet

1

Exercise 10 Conversation practice

A	I say, which	shoe shop / English college	do you go to?

B	I	go to / buy my shoes from	the	one shop college	in the High Street. / near the cinema. / round the corner. / down the road.	Why?

A	I think your	shoes / English	is / are	very	good. / smart.

I'll	go there, too.	
	try that	shop. / college.

B	Yes, do. And	ask for / speak to	my	sister. / father. / friend.	He / She	is the	cashier. / manager.
						works / teaches	there.

Now practise again, but in place of shoes, talk about shirts, trousers and hats. In the place of English, talk about shorthand, typing and French.

Unit 2

I have been waiting for you

The first car has been in the car park since one o'clock.
It has been standing in the car park since one o'clock.
The second car has been in the car park since half past one.
It has been standing in the car park since half past one.
The third car has been here since two o'clock.
It has been standing here since two o'clock.

The first car is Peter's. He is sitting in the cinema now.
He has been sitting in the cinema since one o'clock.
The second car is Margaret's. She is having lunch in a restaurant now.
She has been having lunch since half past one.
The third car is Jillian's mother's. She is shopping now.
She has been shopping since two o'clock.

14

2

Exercise 1

Which car has been standing in the car park for half an hour?
Which car has been standing there for an hour and a half?
Which car has been standing there for an hour?
Who has been sitting in the cinema for an hour and a half?
Who has been shopping for half an hour?
Who has been eating for an hour?
How many cars have been waiting for more than an hour?
How many cars have been waiting for more than a quarter of an hour?
How many cars have been waiting for three quarters of an hour?
How many cars have been waiting for more than two hours?

Exercise 2

Look at the two pictures of the post office and public library on page 7.
Then put these broken sentences together.

The lady with the handbag	has been waiting for a few minutes.
The man with the glasses	has been reading for ten minutes.
The old man with the stick	has been buying something.
The woman sitting in the library	has been phoning his wife every day for weeks.
The man with the telephone	has been talking too long.
The girl behind the library counter	has been buying some flowers.
The little girl with the book	has been going to the same assistant for years.
The little boy's mother	has been asking the boy what he wants.
The young man in the library	has been reading at home.
The man behind the stamp counter	has been writing a letter.

15

2

Exercise 3

Ask somebody:

How long Since when	have you been	learning English? wearing glasses? driving a car? working at the job you have now? smoking? using lipstick? living in the house you have now?

Exercise 4

Look back at the picture of the car park at the beginning of Unit 2. When Peter comes back from the cinema at four o'clock he will have a conversation with the man in the car park:

CAR PARK MAN   Good afternoon, sir.

PETER   Good afternoon. How much do you want?

CAR PARK MAN   Well, your car has been standing there since one o'clock. It's four o'clock now. So it's been standing for three hours. That will be eight pence, please.

PETER   Here you are. I've been seeing that new film. It hasn't been raining, has it?

CAR PARK MAN   Oh no, the sun's been shining. Goodbye, sir.

PETER   Goodbye.

Now make two more conversations: one with Margaret when she comes back from the restaurant at a quarter to three, the other with Jillian's mother when she comes back from shopping at four o'clock. The man in the car park will call them both "Madam".

2

The Valentine card

Saint Valentine's Day is February 14th, and for a very long time young English people have been sending Valentine cards to each other every year. The idea is to tell the other person that you love them, but you never put your name on the card.

One day last February Jillian went into the card shop near her home, a shop which sells many different cards. There were cards for birthdays, Get Well cards for people who are ill, cards saying Congratulations for people who have just had a baby or who have passed an examination, and Valentine cards.

The assistant went across the shop to the cashier.

"I've been selling Valentine cards all day," she said. "People have been coming in and taking two or three. I don't know who they've been buying them for, but the cards have been going very quickly. But that young lady over there," she said, watching Jillian out of the corner of her eye, "hasn't been spending much money. She can't decide what she wants. She's been looking at the cards for half an hour. She's been reading them two or three times; she's been picking them up and putting them down again. And most of the best ones have gone now."

"Most of the best cards have gone now," Jillian thought. "I've been trying to find a good one for Martin for half an hour, but I can't decide." Then suddenly she felt that somebody was watching her. She turned round, but the assistant and the cashier were talking together across the shop. She looked at the big window, and there outside in the street was Susan, Martin's young sister. "Damn," said Jillian to herself. "How long has she been standing there? While I've been trying to find the right card for Martin she has been watching me." She looked down at the Valentine card in her hand. It said:

> "Roses are red, violets are blue.
> Grass is green, and I love you."

"Bah," said Jillian, throwing the card down again onto the counter and walking across the shop to the Get Well cards. That minute Susan came into the shop, went to the Valentine cards, took one to the assistant, and paid for it.

"Hello," she said, walking up to Jillian, "what have you been buying?" But without waiting for an answer, she said in a low voice, "I've just been buying a Valentine card for my favourite man. You've been getting one too, haven't you?"

"Horrible child," Jillian thought to herself. But she said, "No, Susan, I've been looking for a card for a friend who is ill. Here it is." And she picked up the nearest Get Well card and took it to the assistant. "May I have this one, please," she said, "and get me a Valentine card too, please? But do it when that little girl isn't looking."

"She's been reading them all carefully," the assistant told the cashier, "and now she's asked me to decide."

2

2

On February 14th Jillian went to Martin's house.

"Somebody has been thinking about me," he said laughing. "Do you know, I got two cards this morning. And it's St Valentine's Day."

"Two cards!" Jillian said, beginning to feel jealous. "Who has sent him the second card?" she thought. "Two cards, Martin?" she said. "May I see them?"

"Here," Martin said, and Jillian took them. The first was a Valentine card saying:

> "Roses are red, violets are blue.
> Grass is green, and I love you."

"But I didn't send this," she thought, and looked quickly at the second card. It was the Get Well card she bought from the card shop.

"I've been wanting one of those for a long time," Martin said, laughing. "But who do you think sent it? Perhaps it's my boss. He thinks I haven't been working very hard lately. Excuse me, I'll go and get some coffee."

While Martin was in the kitchen, Jillian quickly looked in her handbag. There, next to her lipstick was her Valentine card for Martin.

"And I sent him the wrong one," she thought. Susan came into the room and looked into Jillian's handbag out of the corner of her eye.

"You sent Martin the wrong card, didn't you?" she said. "Shall I tell him the Valentine was from me?" But before Jillian could answer, Susan saw the lipstick. "Ooh, what a nice lipstick. I've been wanting one like that for a long time."

Jillian looked from Susan to the Valentine card, then from the card to her lipstick. Suddenly she took it and gave it to Susan.

"Here," she said, "I have been going to give it to you. I want a new one. And – er – we shan't tell Martin about the cards, shall we?"

New words

a card, a saint, to love, different, congratulations, a baby, to pass, an examination, across, to pick up, damn, while, a rose, a violet, grass, without, lately.

3

Exercise 5

Look at the three pictures in the story.

Picture 1

Who has been looking for a Valentine card?
Who has been standing outside, watching?
Who has been talking about Jillian?
Who has Jillian been thinking about?

Picture 2
Who has been buying a Valentine card?
Who has been looking at Get Well cards?
Who has been laughing?

Picture 3
Who has been looking in Jillian's handbag?
Who has been looking at the cards on the table?
Who has been making coffee?

Exercise 6

Look at the pictures again and answer these questions. Say: "for a long time" or "for a short time".

Picture 1
How long has Jillian been looking at the Valentine cards?
How long has Susan been watching her?
How long has the assistant been talking about her?

Picture 2
How long has Susan been standing in the shop?
How long has the cashier been working in the shop?
How long has Jillian been standing near the Get Well cards?

Picture 3
How long has Jillian been talking to Susan?
How long has Martin been making coffee in the kitchen?
How long has Susan been using lipstick?

Exercise 7
What do you do?

When somebody has been talking about you, do you
(a) ask them why? (b) get angry? (c) talk about them?
When somebody has been watching you, do you
(a) run away? (b) ask them why? (c) begin to watch them?
When somebody says he has been thinking about you, do you feel
(a) angry? (b) glad? (c) silly?

2

1

2

22

2

When somebody has been having a baby, do you say
(a) "Congratulations"? (b) "What are you going to call it?" (c) "I love babies"?
When somebody has been taking an examination, do you
(a) send them a card? (b) buy them a drink? (c) give them a present?
When somebody has been staying in hospital, do you
(a) send them some flowers? (b) send them a Get Well card? (c) write them a letter?
When you think the same person has been sending you Valentine cards for many years, do you
(a) tell them to stop? (b) tell them you are the wrong person? (c) say you will marry them?
When you have been feeling ill for a short time, do you
(a) go to a doctor? (b) tell nobody? (c) have a drink?
When you have been feeling angry for a long time, do you
(a) go to bed? (b) hit something? (c) tell yourself to stop it?
When you have been wanting something for a long time, do you
(a) go and get it? (b) try to forget it? (c) ask somebody to give you it?

Exercise 8

Look at the two pictures of the post office and the library.

The old man began talking at a quarter to three.
The lady at the stamp counter began working in the post office on March 9th.
The man with the telephone began talking to his wife at five minutes to three.
The man at the stamp counter began selling stamps today at nine o'clock.
The girl with the handbag began using this post office in January.
The librarian began working in the library in September.
The little girl began using the children's library last November.
The man with the flowers began taking flowers to the librarian on November 10th.
The lady with the book began reading at twenty minutes past ten.
The man without any hair began wearing glasses when he was twenty.

Now write two new sentences for each of these sentences.
Like this: The old man has been talking since a quarter to three. The old man has been talking for a quarter of an hour.

2

Exercise 9

Ask twelve questions and answer each one.

Has it been raining		reading?
Has the sun been shining	while we have been	working?
Has anybody been smoking		sitting here?
Who has been making a noise		

Exercise 10   Conversation practice

A	I've just been buying	some whisky.
		a lipstick.
		some tobacco.

B	Oh, how long have you been	drinking whisky?
		using lipstick?
		smoking tobacco?

A	I've never	drunk	any before. This is my first.
		used	
		smoked	

A Oh, I'm glad I've seen you. What work have you been doing in college lately?

B Why do you want to know?

A My father thinks I've been learning English, but I've been watching football.

B I can't tell you, because I haven't been going to college this week. I've been swimming. I was going to ask you the same thing.

Now practise again, but in the place of learning English in college, talk about working in the office. In the place of football and swimming, talk about tennis and watching television.

Unit 3

I will help you

Will you marry me?
Yes, I will.
We shall be very happy.

Who will clean the blackboard?
I will, sir.
We all will, sir.
Then I shall clean it myself.

Exercise 1
Practise with somebody.

Ask: Will you {
lend me a pen?
lend me a lot of money?
come swimming with me?
pick up my pencil?
do my work for me?

Answer: Yes, I will. *or* No, I'm sorry, I won't.

Then say:	He She	says	he she	will won't	lend me a pen. lend me a lot of money. come swimming with me. pick up my pencil. do my work for me.

25

3

Exercise 2

Look at the two pictures of the post office and the library on page 22. Which people are saying these sentences?

HE   Will you come to the cinema with me?
SHE   Yes, I will if you give me those flowers.

HE   I haven't any money. Will you give me a stamp?
HE   No, I won't. I shall lose my job if I do.

SHE   Will you lend me your stick?
HE   I'm sorry, but I won't. I can't walk without it.

SHE   I will take this book home and read it in bed.

HE   Yes, I will phone you again tomorrow.

Exercise 3

Answer these questions using either "Yes, I shall" or "Yes, I will".

Will you help anybody who is in trouble?
Will you be glad when you pass your next examination?
Will you be hungry if you don't have any supper tonight?
Will you go to a party if somebody asks you?
Will you use my pen if I give you it?
Will you sleep tonight?
Will you tell me the time, please?
Will you be older next year?

The girl on the roof

One day when the sun was shining and Jillian's office at the B.B.C. was getting warm, she had one of her ideas. "I'll go up onto the roof after lunch," she thought, "and sunbathe. I've been working hard all the morning and I will only stay there for half an hour. But nobody must see me or I shall get into trouble."

So she went onto the high roof, but when she tried to go back to work after half an hour she couldn't open the door again. "Damn," she said, "but what can I do? My boss mustn't know." Then suddenly she knew what to do. She took a pencil and paper from her handbag and wrote a little letter to Martin: "I'm on the B.B.C. roof. Please help me." Then on the other side she wrote: "Will you please take this letter to Mr Martin Fry?" and she wrote the address of Martin's office.

Jillian threw her letter down into the street and saw a man pick it up. He read it, looked up at Jillian and shouted, "Don't worry. I will. I'll take it." So, seeing him walk away with the letter, Jillian lay down again to sunbathe.

1

But what she didn't see was the policeman on the corner of the street, who stopped the man with Jillian's letter.

"Excuse me, sir," he said, "but I've been watching you. Will you show me that piece of paper?"

"Of course I will," the man answered. "But perhaps you will look after it. I'm in a hurry."

The policeman read the paper.

"Certainly I will," he said. "Thank you. I'll look after this." And he went quickly across the road to a telephone box and called the police station.

3

2

"Listen," he said, "there's a young woman on the roof of the B.B.C. I think perhaps she's going to jump off. Will you phone the fire station and tell them to bring their longest ladder? And send an ambulance too."

"Certainly," the police station said. "We will do all that. You stay there. And will you stop cars using that road?"

"Yes, I will," the policeman answered, and left the telephone box.

Five minutes later there were three fire engines and two ambulances outside the B.B.C. Six policemen were stopping people and cars and saying, "Will you please go round? Will you use the next street, please?" A police helicopter was flying low over the roofs and on another roof across the road a clergyman was trying to shout to Jillian.

"Are you there, young lady? Will you listen to me? You won't jump, will you? Don't do anything. We shall be with you in a few minutes."

But London is a noisy place and Jillian could not hear him. While all this was happening she was lying in the sun. "Somebody's making a lot of noise down there," she thought. "But I won't look. I don't want anybody to see me. I'll just lie here and wait for Martin."

And while the policemen and firemen and ambulance men were running about outside the B.B.C., the first policeman was taking Jillian's letter to Martin. "Hello," thought Martin, when he saw the policeman. "Now what have I been doing?"

"Will you come with me please, sir?" the policeman said.

"Oh, I haven't been breaking the law, have I?" Martin asked.

"No, sir, but will you look at this piece of paper? You will come, won't you, sir?" the policeman asked.

"Of course I will," said Martin, jumping up from his desk. "Come on, be quick."

3

When they got back to the B.B.C., everybody was watching the roof.

"We've been trying to get a ladder to her," a fireman told Martin, "but our ladders are all too short." Martin turned to the policeman.

"Listen," he said, "I'm going up to her. But you stay here. I'll go up in the lift."

"What will you say? What will you do?" the policeman asked. But Martin was not listening. He was in the lift, saying to himself, "I must get her down safely. I will get her down safely."

A minute later he pushed open the roof door, and there was Jillian sunbathing.

"Hello, Martin," she said. "Look, I've been getting brown. Thank you for coming, but I couldn't open that silly door. I say, there's a lot of noise down there, isn't there? But I haven't been listening. Now I must go back to my desk. And – er – Martin, you won't tell anybody about this, will you? Or I shall lose my job. Goodbye for now."

Martin stood with his mouth open outside her office door. Then slowly he began to walk down the stairs. In the street outside a car full of newspapermen was stopping and another fire engine with a longer ladder was arriving.

New words

a roof, to sunbathe, of course, to look after, a hurry, certainly, an ambulance, a fire engine, a clergyman.

Exercise 4

Look at the three pictures in the story and answer these questions.

Picture 1
Who has been sunbathing?   Is she still doing it?
Who has been writing?   Is she still doing it?
Who has been walking?   Is he still doing it?
Who has been standing on the corner?   Is he still doing it?

Picture 2
Who has been sunbathing?   Is she still doing it?
Who has been shouting?   Is he still doing it?
What have been arriving?   Are they still doing it?

Picture 3
Who has been smoking a pipe?   Is he still doing it?
Who has been bringing a letter?   Is he still doing it?
Who has been sitting in the office?   Is he still doing it?

3

Exercise 5
Look at the pictures on page 22 and put these broken sentences together.

The young man with the flowers is asking	the man if he will give him a stamp.
The little boy with the letter is asking	her husband if he will phone tomorrow.
The lady at the stamp counter is asking	himself if she will ever turn round.
The man without any hair is asking	the librarian if she will go to the cinema.
The wife speaking on the telephone is asking	the old man if he will lend her his stick.

Exercise 6
Now look at the pictures in the story again and read these sentences.

Picture 1
Jillian's letter is telling the man to take it to Martin.
The letter is telling Martin to come and help her.
The policeman is going to tell the man to show him the letter.

Picture 2
The clergyman has told Jillian to listen to him.
He is telling her to stay there quietly.
The policeman is telling the car driver to use another street.
He is telling him to go round the corner.

Picture 3
The policeman has told Martin to go with him.
He is going to tell Martin to read the letter.
Martin is going to tell him to be quick.

Now write the sentences again, but in place of "to tell" use "to ask if he will".
Like this: Jillian's letter is telling the man to take it to Martin. Jillian's letter is asking the man if he will take it to Martin.
Your new sentences will be like those in Exercise 5.

3

Exercise 7

Jillian said to Martin, "You won't tell anybody about this, will you?"
And the policeman said to Martin, "You will come, won't you?" Now
practise with a friend.

May I borrow your	
Will you lend me your	address book.
Please show me your	

Of course. Certainly.	But you'll give me it back soon, won't you? But you won't keep it long, will you? But you won't show it to anybody, will you? But you'll be careful with it, won't you?

Practise again, but ask for a lipstick, a cigarette case, examination papers
and holiday photographs.

Exercise 8

Jillian said to herself,
   "I'll go up on the roof." I'll = I will.
The man at the beginning of this Unit said,
   "We shall be very happy." We shall = We'll.
Now here are some sentences from the story. Write them again using
"I'll", "We'll" or "You'll".

I will only stay there for half an
   hour.
I shall get into trouble.
Perhaps you will look after it.
I will look after this.
We will do all that.

We shall be with you in a few
   minutes.
You will come, won't you, sir?
I will get her down safely.
I shall lose my job.

3

Exercise 9
Finish these sentences.

I shall not be in a hurry tomorrow if I leave home at — .
I shall be — on my next birthday.
For my next holidays I shall go to — .
For breakfast tomorrow I shall have — .
I shall be in — at half past eleven tonight.
I will buy my friend a — if I have the money.
I will tell you my — if you will tell me yours.
I will not dance with anybody who — .
I will not sunbathe when the sun — .
I will try to — if you help me.

Exercise 10   Conversation practice

A	Excuse me,	sir, madam,	but will you do something for me?

B	Of course, Certainly,	I will if I can. What is it?

A	I've dropped my	money glasses	somewhere and I can't see	it. them.

B	Oh,	it's they're	here, look. You've been	sitting standing	on	it. them.

Practise again, but in place of money and glasses, use tickets and tobacco.

Unit 4

So am I

Here are Tim, Tony and Susan.
The boys are standing and so is Susan.
Susan is looking at the ball and so are the boys.
Tim has one sister and so has Tony.
Susan has one older brother and so have the boys.

Exercise 1

Look at the pictures on page 35. Then finish these sentences.

An old man is standing at the counter and so is — .
A lady is sitting behind the counter and so are — .
The man with the telephone is talking and so is — .
The old man has something in his hand and so has — .
The man with the glasses has a book and so have — and — .
The library assistant is happy and so is — .
The young man is holding something and so are — and — .
Two men have come to the library and so have — and — .

Now talk about yourself and other people.

I am		wearing —			am I.
He	is	looking at —		is	he.
She		near —	and so		she.
		feeling —			
You	are	— years old		are	you.
They					they.

4

1

2

4

Nor am I

Look again at Tim,
Tony and Susan.

The boys aren't holding the ball and nor is Susan.
Susan isn't sitting and nor are the boys.
Tim hasn't got a hat on and nor have the others.
Tim and Tony haven't seen Martin and nor has Susan.

Exercise 2
Look at these three pictures again.

4

Picture 1
The two assistants are in the shop and so is — .
Jillian isn't looking at the birthday cards and nor is — .
The assistants haven't seen Susan and nor has — .
Susan has been watching Jillian and so have — .

Picture 2
Susan has picked up a card and so has — .
Jillian hasn't paid the cashier yet and nor has — .
The cashier has been laughing at Jillian and so has — .

Picture 3
Jillian is at Martin's house and so are — and — .
The Valentine card is on the table and so is — .
Susan isn't going to tell Martin who sent the cards and nor is — .

Now talk about yourself and other people.

I am								am I.
			thinking about my work					
He	is		a good driver			so	is	he.
She		(not)	too warm	and		nor		she.
			going to bed early tonight					
You	are		a heavy smoker				are	you.
They								they.

He	has			been to the cinema today				has	he.
She				had a birthday this year			so		she.
			(n't)	read a lot of books	and		nor		
I				been reading a lot lately					I.
You	have			got a shower at home				have	you.
They									they.

4

So do I

Martin likes beer and so does Jillian.
Martin doesn't smoke cigarettes and
nor does Jillian.

Exercise 3

Find somebody who does the same as you do.

Ask: Do you spend a lot of money on
- food?
- drink?
- tobacco?
- clothes?

After their answer say: Yes, so do I. *or* No, nor do I.

Ask: Do you like
- roses?
- babies?
- examinations?
- music?

After their answer say: Yes, so do I. *or* No, nor do I.
Now tell another person.

I	spend don't spend	a lot of money on	food drink tobacco clothes

and	so nor	does —— . do —— and —— .

I	like don't like	roses babies examinations music	and	so nor	does —— . do —— and —— .

4

The man with the encyclopaedia

Jillian and Martin were out in the car one evening.

"Do you know, Martin," Jillian said, "I've had a man who tried to sell me an encyclopaedia."

"That's funny," Martin answered, "so have I. Perhaps it was the same salesman. Mine had brown hair and a moustache."

"So had mine," Jillian said. "And he couldn't say his 'r's properly."

"Nor could mine," said Martin smiling. "It must be the same man. He came last night. But I was rather annoyed."

"Yes, so was I, Martin. He knocked on my door one evening last week, came in and sat down and started talking like an old friend. He was selling twenty-four encyclopaedias."

"So was the man who came to see me," Martin said, "but I shan't buy them."

"Nor shall I," said Jillian. "I can't afford them, and nor can you, I'm sure."

"You're right, there," Martin said, stopping the car and putting his arm round Jill's shoulder. "But I want to know who gave this salesman my name and address."

"And so do I," said Jillian. "I've been trying to think all day who did, but I haven't the faintest idea." They were quiet for a minute. Then Jillian said, "What are you thinking about?"

"Well, to tell you the truth," Martin said, "I'm feeling rather guilty."

"That's funny," Jillian said, turning to him, "so am I. You see, when I told the encyclopaedia man I didn't want his books, he asked me for the name and address of a friend who reads a lot. So I gave him Peter and Liz Smith's address."

"Oh," said Martin, putting his hands over his face, "so did I. And I've been feeling guilty about it ever since."

"Yes, I have, too, Martin," Jillian said. "Shall we go and tell them he's coming?"

"You're very sweet," Martin said, kissing the end of her nose, and starting the car at the same time.

4

"We won't say we both gave the salesman their address," Martin said, as he rang the Smiths' door bell. "I'll tell Peter I sent him. And perhaps he hasn't been here yet."

Peter came to the door. "Look who's here," he called to Liz. "Come in, you two."

When they were all sitting down, Jillian began to tell their story. "I've had a man trying to sell me some encyclopaedias," she said, "and so has Martin."

Peter threw his head back, laughing. "So have we," he said. "He was a young man with brown hair and a moustache who couldn't say his 'r's properly."

"Yes, so was ours," Martin answered, looking guiltily at Jillian. "It was the same man."

Liz said, "Of course we couldn't afford them."

"No, I couldn't either," Jillian said, "and nor could Martin. But we were both very annoyed."

"Yes, so were we," Peter said. "He walked in here like an old friend of the family and sat down and started talking. I felt very angry with him and so did Liz, didn't you?"

Martin looked across at Jillian. "She's feeling uncomfortable," he thought, "and so am I. We must tell Peter and Liz that we gave the man their address."

"It's funny," he began, "we haven't the faintest idea why he came to us. But before he left he asked both of us for the name and address of a friend who reads a lot."

But before he could finish, Peter threw back his head again, laughing noisily. "Oh, did he? And you gave him somebody's name, did you? So did we. We gave him yours, Martin, and yours, Jill."

"Yes," Liz said, "and I've been feeling guilty for the last two weeks."

4

"Two weeks?" Jillian said, looking up quickly. "So it was you who sent him to us."

"Yes, but I didn't think he was going to come," Peter said, "and nor did Liz."

"Don't worry," Martin said, smiling and looking at the clock. "I'm sorry, but I must go and so must Jill."

As they were going out of the Smiths' front door Peter asked "Oh, you haven't told us. Whose address did you give the man?"

Jillian smiled. "Why, you gave your best friends' names, and so did we. We told him to come here."

They were getting into the car when another car stopped outside the Smiths' house. The driver was another young man and he had a box of encyclopaedias with him.

"Oh look, Jill," Martin laughed. "The other salesman didn't get any money out of Liz and Peter, and nor will he."

"No, he won't," said Jillian, uncomfortably as they drove away, "but whose names do you think Peter will give this man?"

New words

an encyclopaedia, funny, a salesman, a moustache, properly, to smile, rather, annoyed, to afford, a shoulder, faint, truth, guilty, sweet, to kiss, guiltily, noisily, whose.

Exercise 4

Finish these sentences, using "so" or "nor".

Martin's man had brown hair and a moustache and — — Jillian's.
Martin's man couldn't say his "r"s properly and — — Jillian's.
Martin was rather annoyed with him and — — Jillian.
Martin couldn't afford to buy the books and — — Jillian.
Martin didn't buy any books and — — Jillian.
Martin didn't know who sent him and — — Jillian.
Martin gave the man the Smiths' address and — — Jillian.
Martin and Jillian were both annoyed with the man and — — Peter and Liz.
Martin and Jillian both felt guilty about giving a friend's name and — — Liz.
Peter didn't laugh when the second encyclopaedia man arrived, and — — Liz.

4

Exercise 5

Here is the conversation between Peter and the second encyclopaedia man.

MAN   Good evening, Mr Smith. May I come in and show you some wonderful new books?

PETER   Oh, good evening. Are you trying to sell me something?

MAN   Well, yes. But I'm sure you have never seen any encyclopaedias as good as these before.

PETER   I'm sorry, but another man was here the other day with the same books and they were too expensive for me. We couldn't afford them. Goodbye.

MAN   Oh, very well. Goodbye.

Now make a new conversation between yourself and a lady selling lipsticks, which you don't like. Then another conversation with a man selling flowers, which you don't want. (You bought some yesterday from another man, whose flowers were cheaper.)

Exercise 6

In the story, Jillian said, "Yes, I have, too," and "No, I couldn't either."

"I have, too" is the same as "so have I".
"I couldn't either" is the same as "nor could I".

Now write this part of the story, but in the place of "so — —" and "nor — —" use "— — too" and "–n't, either".

"Mine has brown hair and a moustache."
"So had mine," Jillian said. "And he couldn't say his 'r's properly."
"Nor could mine," said Martin, smiling. "It must be the same man. But I was rather annoyed."
"Yes, so was I, Martin. He was selling twenty-four encyclopaedias."
"So was the man who came to see me," Martin said. "But I shan't buy them."
"Nor shall I," said Jillian. "I can't afford them, and nor can you, I'm sure."

4

Exercise 7

Ask ten questions and give ten true answers.

If,	tomorrow, next week,	somebody a man	tries to sell you some

encyclopaedias,	how will you feel?
cheap cigarettes,	what will you do?
plastic flowers,	what will you say?

I shall feel rather $\begin{cases} \text{annoyed.} \\ \text{glad.} \end{cases}$ I won't $\begin{cases} \text{buy any.} \\ \text{say anything.} \end{cases}$

I'll tell him $\begin{cases} \text{to — .} \\ \text{that — .} \end{cases}$

Exercise 8

Read the story again, then answer these questions.

Whose house did the encyclopaedia man go to first?
Whose house did he go to second?
Whose house did he go to last?
Whose house did the second encyclopaedia man go to?
Whose address did Peter give the first man?
Whose address did Martin give him?
Whose address did Jillian give him?
Whose address will you give him if he comes to your house?

Exercise 9

Go back to the story in Unit 3 about Jillian on the roof. Read it again and finish these sentences, using either "so" or "nor".

The man in the street read Jillian's letter and — — the policeman.
The man didn't know she was sunbathing and — — the policeman.
Two ambulances arrived and — — three fire engines.
The firemen could not get to Jillian and — — the clergyman.

4

The clergyman and the cars were making a lot of noise and — — the helicopter.

The policeman didn't use the lift and — — the firemen.

While the policeman was going to Martin the other policemen were running about and — — — the ambulance men.

Jillian won't tell her boss about going on the roof and — — Martin.

The newspapermen were too late and — — the last fire engine.

Exercise 10   Conversation practice

| A | Whose is this old | birthday
Valentine
Congratulations
Get Well | card? |

| B | I don't know.
I've no idea.
I haven't the faintest idea. |

| A | No, I don't either.
Nor do I.
No, I haven't either.
Nor have I. | I'll throw it away. |

| B | No, | give it to me.
I'll have it. | I'll send it to you |

for your birthday next year.
next St Valentine's day.
after your next examination.
the next time you are ill.

Unit 5

The man who is climbing
The rope which is too short
The man whose hat is falling

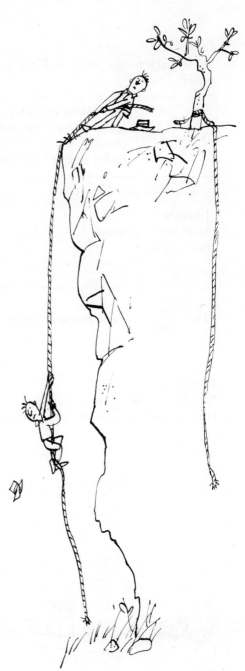

Here are two men on a mountain.
One man is pulling the rope. He is
   at the top.
The other man is climbing the rope.
   He has lost his hat.
Which man is at the top?
The man who is pulling the rope is
   at the top.
Which man has lost his hat?
The man who is climbing the rope
   has lost his hat.
There are two ropes.
One rope goes round the tree. That
   is the shorter rope.
The other rope goes round the top
   man. That is the longer rope.
Which rope is the shorter?
The rope which goes round the tree
   is the shorter.
Which rope is the longer?
The rope which goes round the top
   man is the longer.
Each man has a hat.
One is on the grass at the top and
   one is falling.
Which man is climbing and which
   man is holding the rope?
The man whose hat is falling is
   climbing the rope.
The man whose hat is on the grass
   is holding the rope.

5

Exercise 1

Think back to the story in Unit 4. How many true sentences can you write?

A man who	was selling encyclopaedias had a moustache and brown hair couldn't say his "r"s had a box of books in his car	went to

Jillian's Martin's the Smiths'	house.

The	one ones	whose house he came to	first second last	was were	Jillian. Martin. Peter and Liz.

Exercise 2

Now look at these three pictures again.
How many true sentences can you make?

1   2

5

3

The	picture which shows pictures which show	most people Jill's letter the B.B.C. roof an ambulance cars Martin

is are	the first. the second. the third. the first and the third. the first and the second. the second and the third.

The rope he is climbing

Look again at the two men with the two ropes.

The top man has fastened one round the tree.
Which is the rope he has fastened round the tree?
The shorter one is the rope he has fastened round the tree.
Which is the rope he is holding?
The longer one is the rope he is holding.
And it is the rope the other man is climbing.

5

Exercise 3
Say to somebody:

You've spoken to some people today. Who was the first person you spoke to?
You've eaten things today. What was the first thing you ate?
You've done some work today. What was the hardest work you did?
You like doing some things. What is the thing you like doing most?
You don't like doing some things. What are the things you don't like doing?
You don't like some people. Who are the people you don't like?
You like some people. Who are the people you like most?
You will do many things tomorrow. What is the thing you will do first?
You want to go to many places. Which is the place you want to go to most?
You are wearing clothes. What are some of the things you are wearing?

Exercise 4
Finish these sentences.
e.g. Salesmen who sell books at your door are a nuisance. The books they sell are often expensive.

Salesmen who sell books at your door are — . The books they sell are — .
One man who usually wears a helmet is a — . The helmet he wears is — .
People who buy expensive clothes go shopping at — . The clothes they buy are — .
Women who smoke cigarettes — . The cigarettes they smoke — .
A friend who writes to me — . The letters she writes — .
Men who drink and then drive — . The passengers they carry — .

At the launderette

"Do you know a good place where I can take my washing?" Martin asked Jillian one day.

"Why, yes," she told him. "Mrs Brass, the woman who cleans for us, takes all my washing to the launderette in the High Street. You know, Martin, the one which is next door to the do-it-yourself shop."

48

"Ah, yes, I know," said Martin, "I'll try it. I'm going there this afternoon for some glue I want. Thanks very much."

Later that afternoon Martin walked into the launderette. In one hand he had a briefcase which held his dirty washing, in the other was a packet of glue powder he bought next door. For a moment he stood and watched the line of washing machines which stood against the wall, and the people who were using them. One machine was free, so Martin put his briefcase on it and slowly began to take out his washing and his packet of soap powder. All the time he watched the two women who were using the machines on each side of him. The big, middle-aged woman who was on his left was emptying her packet of soap powder into her machine, but the younger woman who was on Martin's right was just starting, so he tried to learn from her.

WASH ···· 10p

DRY ···· 3p

When she put in her soap powder and the first lot of clothes she wanted to wash, so did Martin. When she put her money into her machine, so did Martin in his. And when hers filled itself with water, so did Martin's.

He smiled gently to himself as the machine began to work. At that moment the middle-aged woman whose machine was on Martin's left

5

walked out of the launderette. As she went past him, she knocked his briefcase and the packet of glue powder fell to the floor and broke open.

"Oh dear," he thought, "I mustn't make a mess. And I can't carry it home like that. What can I do?" Then he saw the middle-aged woman's empty soap powder packet which was still on top of her machine. "She's finished with it," he thought, "and she was the one who knocked my glue onto the floor." He looked quickly out of the corner of his eye to the next machine where the younger woman was watching her clothes. Nobody was looking, so he took the older woman's empty packet, and it was the work of a moment to empty the glue powder into it from the broken packet.

It was still in his hand when the middle-aged woman came back, stopped her washing machine and emptied it. In a bag she had another lot of clothes she was going to wash, and as she filled her machine again she turned and saw the soap packet Martin was still holding.

"Here," she said, "that's the packet I left on my machine when I went out."

"But it was empty," Martin said, looking guilty, "and . . ."

"Empty?" she answered, in a voice which made everybody turn to look. "What do you think this is?" And before Martin could speak, she emptied his glue powder into her machine and dropped her money in to start it. "I don't like people who take other people's things," she said between her teeth.

"I'm sorry, madam," Martin said, "but I don't think you know what you have done." At that moment Martin's machine switched itself off and as he took out his clothes, she stood over him and shouted, "Oh, I don't know what I've done, don't I? I know what you've done. You've taken the soap powder I left on my machine. You've used the powder I've paid for. And that's the truth."

Trying not to look guilty, Martin pushed his clothes back into his briefcase, while the woman whose machine was full of glue began to tell her story to the other women who were there.

At that moment he heard Jillian's voice behind him. "Ah, Martin, have you been having a good time?" Then Jill turned to the angry middle-aged woman who was still throwing her arms about. "Hello, Mrs Brass," she said, "have you finished my washing?"

"Oh, hello, Miss Grey. No, I've done mine. I'm doing yours now." Martin looked quickly through the glass window in the front of Mrs Brass's machine where Jillian's clothes were going round slowly in a thick grey mess.

5

He took Jillian's shoulder and turned her round quickly away from the women who were watching.

"Jill," he said, "there's something I want to tell you. But not here. Come somewhere where we can talk." And he pushed her gently out of the launderette, towards the coffee shop, as Mrs Brass turned to see why the machine she was using was not working properly.

New words
a launderette, a briefcase, a packet, powder, a moment, against, middle-aged, to empty, gently, a tooth, thick.

Exercise 5
Read the story again and ask somebody these questions.

Whose house does Mrs Brass clean?
Whose washing machine was next to Mrs Brass's?
Whose machine was on Martin's right?
Whose machine was on his left?
Whose packet broke open?
Whose packet did Martin put the glue into?
Whose clothes were in Mrs Brass's second washing bag?
Whose voice did Martin hear behind him?
Whose shoulder did Martin put his hand on?
Whose washing machine was not working properly?

Exercise 6
Here is a list of places.

a restaurant, a library, a college, a supermarket, a launderette, a kitchen, a railway station, a post office, a bathroom, a bowling alley, a tennis court.

Ask: Which one is the place where we may borrow books?
Answer: A library.

Now ask ten more questions about the other places. Start your questions:
Which one is the place where — ?

5

Exercise 7

Here is a list of people.

a postman, a magician, a secretary, a nurse, a cashier, a passenger, a detective, a pilot, a manager, a librarian, a weather forecaster.

Ask: Which one is the person who looks after people when they are ill?
Answer: A nurse.

Now ask ten more questions about the other people. Start your questions: Which one is the person who — ?

And here is another list of people.

a doctor, a secretary, an actor, a teacher, a policeman, a hairdresser, a driver, a tennis player, a train cleaner, a window cleaner, a man who sells dictionaries.

Ask: Which one is the person whose work is in a hospital?
Answer: A doctor.

Now ask ten more questions about the other people. Start your questions: Which one is the person whose work — ?

Exercise 8

Here is a list of eleven things.

money, a pair of scissors, a handbag, a toothbrush, a washing machine, a mouth, a bat, a pencil, an electric beater, a hand, a coffee machine.

Ask: Which one is the thing which buys things?
Answer: Money.

Now ask ten more questions about the others. Ask: Which one is the thing which — things?

5

And here is another list of things.

a camera, a scarf, a taxi, a diary, a violin, a dictionary, a ladder, a bath-plug, a pipe, a glove, a shoe-lace.

Ask: Which one is the thing people take photographs with?
Answer: A camera.

Now ask ten more questions about the others. Start your questions: Which one is the thing people — ?

Exercise 9
Look at the picture in the story and write sentences about:
the young woman who is walking across the launderette
the woman who is behind Martin
the briefcase which is on the second machine
the bag which is against the first machine
the woman at the back whose face we can't see
the woman whose soap packet is on her machine
the machine Martin is using
the packet Martin has put on his machine
the place where the man is sitting
the wall where the notice is

Exercise 10   Conversation practice

A	Do you know a	shop place	where I can	get buy	some good coffee?

B	Yes. Many people I	know talk to like	get theirs at the shop which is		

near		cinema.
next door to	the	launderette.
just past		ambulance station.

5

| A | Thanks. Was | this
that | coffee | I've just drunk
you've just given me
you made last night
we had at your party | from there? |

| B | Certainly not. I can't afford to | use
buy |

| | coffee from the shop | I've just told you about.
my friends go to. |

Now practise again, but in place of coffee talk about wine, cake and face powder.

Unit 6

The one which went
The one that went

Here are three packets of cigarettes.
The one that is the most expensive is on the right.
The cigarettes that are the cheapest are on the left.
The packet that costs fifteen pence is in the middle.

that = which

Exercise 1
Look at the three packets of cigarettes again. How many true sentences
can you make?

	Pilot		is made in America.
	Three Bells		has a man on the front.
The	New York	packet is the one that	is in the middle.
	smallest		is on the left.
	biggest		is on the right.

Exercise 2
Ask somebody:

When you buy a book, do you get
(a) one that is easy to understand or one that is hard to understand?
(b) one that makes you laugh or one that makes you cry?

When you go to see a film, do you like
(a) one that has a lot of music in it or one that has a lot of love in it?
(b) one that makes you think or one that stops you thinking?
When you ride in a car, do you like
(a) one that can't go very fast or one that can go very fast?
(b) one that uses a lot of petrol or one that doesn't use much petrol?
When you have a holiday, do you like
(a) one that takes you away from people or one that puts you with a lot of people?
(b) one that makes you travel a lot or one that doesn't?

Exercise 3
Write ten true sentences.

I	get rather annoyed by get angry with rather like love laugh at	people books films writers television programmes	who that	are hard to understand. tell me what to do. make me feel guilty. try to help me. don't tell the truth.

Exercise 4
Peter Smith works for an advertising agent. He writes advertisements, but his boss always writes them again in a different way. They were advertising some new houses and Peter wrote: "These houses are the cheapest."
But his boss wrote: "These are the houses that are the cheapest."
Now read what Peter wrote, then write what his boss wrote. (His boss always starts: "These are the houses that — .")

These houses make you feel at home.
These houses will still be here in 2050.
These houses will never look old.
These houses are the easiest to buy.
These houses laugh at bad weather.
These houses have two bathrooms.
These houses will make your friends jealous.
These houses are the easiest to clean.

Exercise 5

Then Peter wrote some more advertisements and his boss changed them again. Peter wrote: "Everybody likes these houses."
But his boss wrote: "These are the houses everybody likes."
Read what Peter wrote and then write the new sentences his boss wrote. (His boss always starts: "These are the houses — .")

The smartest people buy these houses.
You will want to live in these houses.
Everybody can afford these houses.
Nobody can forget these houses.
People never want to leave these houses.
Children love these houses.
The sun always shines on these houses.
You have been waiting for these houses.
You have seen these houses on television.
People call them the houses of the future.

Mrs Brass and the pop record

Jillian lives in a flat in a house in London, but it is very expensive, so she shares the flat she lives in with two other girls, Christina and Philippa. They share the expenses, too. One week Jillian gives the money that pays for the food and Christina and Philippa pay for the cleaning and the rent. The next week Jillian gives the money that pays for the cleaning and Christina and Philippa pay for the rent and the food. The third week, Jillian pays the rent and the other two give the money that pays for the cleaning and the food. And they are all very happy.

Another time when they share expenses is when they have a party. So they all pay for the drink they give their friends, the food they all eat and for the work Mrs Brass does.

The three girls decided to give a party one evening last winter. An hour before it was going to start, Philippa was looking through a pile of records that lay on the living-room carpet. Christina was cleaning her teeth in the bathroom with Philippa's new toothpaste. And Jillian was running from room to room shouting, "Has anybody seen my blouse? The one that went in the glue?"

6

There was the noise of a plate breaking in the kitchen, and Mrs Brass put her head round the door. "That's the second one I've broken, Miss Grey. Every time you say something that makes me think of the launderette, I drop something."

At that moment, Philippa switched the record-player on and the noise that filled the living-room sent Mrs Brass back into the kitchen.

"Do they call that music?" she said loudly as she dried another plate. Then she looked again at Philippa dancing in the middle of the living-room carpet. "Silly young things, throwing themselves about on the carpet I've just cleaned," said Mrs Brass in a loud voice, but Philippa didn't hear what she said.

6

But the music that was making Philippa dance was filling Mrs Brass's head, too. So while Philippa stopped dancing for a moment to listen to the record, it was Mrs Brass who began to turn and shake her shoulders to the music behind the kitchen door.

"What's that record?" Jillian asked, fastening the buttons of her blouse as she came into the living-room.

The record player switched itself off, and Philippa picked up the record and put another one on.

"It's that pop group that was on the television last week," she said. "Look."

Jillian read the label on the record and laughed loudly. "Beat the Floor with Benny's Brass," she read. Then Christina came in.

"That was Benny's Brass that was playing, wasn't it?" she said. "But why are you laughing, Jill?"

"Sh," Jillian said. "Don't you know? Mrs Brass calls her husband Benny. So she's Benny's Brass, too. No, please be quiet, you two; she'll be annoyed if she hears what we're saying." As she spoke, Mrs Brass came out of the kitchen with some glasses and bottles and put them on a table that stood between the record-player and the fireplace.

But as she did so, she knocked Jillian's hand that held the record, and it flew into the fire. Christina tried to get it, but she was too late. For a moment, nobody spoke, then Mrs Brass put a hand up to her red face, saying "Oh dear, it's not my good day. It's a good thing it was only a little pop record." And she went back to the kitchen.

"That's the record I bought this morning," Philippa said. "It was Benny's Brass."

"Yes," said Jillian slowly. "But did Mrs Brass know?"

"You mean you think she heard us laughing at Benny's Brass," Christina asked, "and then knocked the record into the fire deliberately?"

"I'm not sure," Jillian said in a low voice. "It's not easy to know what she thinks. She often says things she doesn't mean."

Mrs Brass came out of the kitchen with her coat on. "I'm going now," she said. "The cups and saucers that are on the kitchen table are for the coffee. Have a nice party." And she went.

Later in the evening when the three girls were dancing with their boy-friends, the door bell rang. "Oh, answer it for me, Martin," Jillian said, "while I see what the coffee's doing."

Martin came back a moment later with Mrs Brass. She gave Jillian something that was in a paper packet. "I have been worrying about that

6

record that fell into the fire," she said. "Will you borrow this one I bought yesterday?"

"But that's much better. It's a long-playing record," said Philippa, "and ours that fell into the fire was only a little one."

"What's its name?" Christina asked. "Look at the label."

Jillian took the record and read, "Benny's Brass Goes to a Party. Benny's Brass," she laughed. "So you knew all the time. And you like pop music. Come on, everybody. We'll drink to Benny's Brass. Have a drink, Mrs Brass."

"To Benny's Brass who make music," said the men.

"And to Benny's Brass who cleans for us." answered the three girls. And they all drank.

"Thank you," Mrs Brass said. "But now I must go back to my Benny. Goodnight."

New words

pop, a record, a flat, to share, expenses, rent, a winter, a pile, toothpaste, a record-player, loudly, a group, a label, brass, a fireplace, to mean, deliberately, a saucer, long-playing, goodnight.

The girl who is dancing near the table
The girl dancing near the table

Exercise 6

Look at the picture in the story and say:

That's Philippa who is dancing in the living-room.
That's Mrs Brass who is washing up in the kitchen.
That's Benny's Brass that is playing on the record.
Those are pop records that are lying on the carpet.
That's a record-player that is standing against the wall.

Now do it again, but don't say "who is", etc. Say it like this:
That's Philippa dancing in the living-room.

Now use those sentences again and say:
I can see Philippa dancing in the living-room, etc.

6

Exercise 7

Look at the picture
of the car park again.

Peter's car has been there the longest time. So, is Peter's car
(a) the car that is standing on the left,
(b) the one standing in the middle,
(c) the one on the right?

Margaret left her car in the park at 1.30. So, is Margaret's car
(a) the car that is waiting next to Jillian's mother's,
(b) the one waiting next but one to Jillian's mother's,
(c) the one next but two to Jillian's mother's?

Jillian's mother parked her car at 2.00. So, is hers
(a) the car that has been standing there the longest time,
(b) the car that has been there the shortest time?

Whose is the car that has been waiting in the park for an hour?
Whose is the car that has been in the park for half an hour?
Whose is the car that has been there for an hour and a half?

6

Exercise 8

Read the story again, then without looking, try to remember:

While Christina was cleaning her teeth, what was Philippa looking through?

While Jillian was running from room to room, what was she looking for?

When Philippa switched the record player on, what sent Mrs Brass back into the kitchen?

When the girls dance, what does Mrs Brass say they do?

Which group did Philippa tell Jillian was playing on her new record?

When Mrs Brass carried some bottles and glasses into the living-room, what did she put them on?

What did Philippa say when the record fell into the fire?

What record did Mrs Brass lend Jillian?

Who did the men drink to?

Who did the girls drink to?

Exercise 9

Here are two sentences.

Christina was using Philippa's toothpaste. Did Philippa know?

We can say: Did Philippa know what Christina was using?

Make one question like that from each of these pairs of sentences and ask somebody.

Mrs Brass dropped a plate. Did Jillian see?

Mrs Brass dropped a plate. Did Jillian hear?

Mrs Brass said something about dancing. Did Philippa hear?

Mrs Brass calls her husband Benny. Did Christina know?

The girls were saying things about Mrs Brass. Did Mrs Brass hear?

Christina thought Mrs Brass dropped the record deliberately. Did Mrs Brass know?

Mrs Brass brought something to the flat. Did Jillian like it?

Something was on the label of the new record. Did Martin read it?

6

Exercise 10   Conversation practice

A	Is there one	person thing	who that	always makes you	laugh? smile?

B	Yes, that man who	writes tells	funny stories	on the	television. radio.
				in the newspaper.	

A	But he	doesn't feel never feels	happy, you know. I met him last	spring. summer. autumn. winter.

B	Then why does he deliberately	tell write	stories	

that make people laugh? people think are funny?

A	He's trying all the time to make himself	happy. laugh.	But he can't.

Unit 7

Less milk and fewer bottles
The least milk and the fewest bottles

Jillian, Liz and Alison have been to the supermarket. Look at the milk they have bought.

Jillian has bought a little milk, Liz has got more milk and Alison has got the most milk.

Alison has got a lot of milk, Liz has got less milk and Jillian has got the least milk.

Jillian has bought one bottle, Liz has got more bottles and Alison has got the most bottles.

Alison has got a few bottles, Liz has got fewer bottles and Jillian has got the fewest.

Exercise 1

Ask somebody:

Who has bought the least tea? Who has bought the most? Who has bought less tea than Alison?

Who has bought the fewest packets of tea? Who has bought the most? Who has bought fewer packets of tea than Liz?

Who has bought the most fish? Who has bought the least? Who has bought less fish than Jillian?

Who has bought the most meat? Who has bought the least? Who has bought less meat than Alison?

Who has bought the most pieces of meat? Who has bought the fewest pieces of meat? Who has bought fewer pieces than Liz?

7

Exercise 2
Write five correct sentences.

People who want to get thinner must	eat drink

less fewer	sweet things.
	bread.
	sandwiches.
	sugar.
	cakes.
	glasses of whisky.
	whisky.

Exercise 3
When Jillian, Liz and Alison came out of the supermarket, they had this conversation.

JILL   I say, Alison, you've spent a lot of money.

ALISON   Yes, and I think I've bought too much milk.

JILL   Oh, I've bought less than you, but perhaps I've got too little.

LIZ   Yes, you took the least milk of the three of us, Jill. But if you've got too little and Alison's got too much, buy some of hers. Then you'll both be happy.

JILL   What a good idea!

Now practise the conversation again, but in the place of milk, talk about bottles of milk. Then practise again with fish, and then with tins of fish. (But first look carefully at the pictures at the beginning of this Unit.)

7

I ran more quickly
You ran the most quickly

Peter drives slowly.

Martin drives more quickly.

Tom drives the most quickly.

7

Exercise 4

Ask somebody:

Who drives	carefully? more dangerously? the most dangerously? the most carefully?	Peter, Martin or Tom?

Whose passenger is riding	comfortably? more uncomfortably? the most uncomfortably?	Peter's, Martin's or Tom's?

Exercise 5

Look again at the three drivers and their passengers. Then answer these questions.

Does Martin drive more slowly than Tom?
Does Martin drive more slowly than Peter?
Does Martin drive the most slowly?
Does Martin drive the most carefully?
Does Martin drive more quickly than Tom?
Does Martin drive more carefully than Peter?
Does Jillian ride more comfortably than Mary does behind Tom?
Does Jillian ride the most comfortably?
Does Jillian ride more uncomfortably than Liz does behind Peter?
Does Jillian ride the most safely?

1

2

7

Exercise 6

Look at these two pictures again, and put these broken sentences together.

The woman reading a book is	standing more uncomfortably than the library assistant.
The woman carrying a handbag is	waiting more angrily than the woman with the book.
The young man with the flowers is	walking more slowly than the little girl.
The little boy with a letter is	sitting more comfortably than the post office assistants.
The man whose glasses are falling is	working more helpfully than the library assistant.
The lady assistant in the post office is	talking more happily than the old man with the stick.

Now say who you think is talking the most noisily, talking the most gently, talking the most excitedly, looking after something the most carefully, looking after something the most carelessly.

A holiday for Martin's grandparents

"The older I get," said Martin's grandmother, carefully watching Jillian put a second spoonful of sugar into her cup, "the less sugar I want in my tea." Jillian quickly stopped herself from taking a third spoonful and smiled.

She and Martin were visiting his grandparents, and as usual when they went there, they were not sure what to talk about.

"There's been less rain this week," Martin said. His grandfather came into the living-room and put a hand to his ear.

"What's that you say?" he asked.

"We've had fewer rainy days," Martin said more loudly. "More sun and fewer showers."

"Oh yes," the old man said. "It's funny. Your grandmother and I have been talking lately about that. We've been looking for somewhere to spend our holidays. Some place that has the most sunny days and the least wind."

"Of course," Martin's grandmother said, gently taking the sugar bowl away from Jillian's side. "Of course at our age we have the most time but the least money for holidays. But we've been thinking about Dover and Bournemouth, and about Windermere, too."

"Oh why does she always talk about how little money they've got?" Martin thought. "We must talk about their holidays." And he looked hard at Jillian.

She understood. "Oh," she said, sitting back more comfortably, "that's interesting. But you'll get the fewest cold days at Bournemouth, won't you? I'm sure it has less wind than Dover and most certainly Windermere has the least fine weather of those three."

"What's she say?" asked Martin's grandfather again.

"She says Bournemouth has the least wind and Windermere has the most bad weather," his wife said.

"Hm," said grandfather, "when we visited Bournemouth in the summer of nineteen-fifty-five it rained more heavily than usual and I saw more television in one week than I've seen since."

"And you spent more money on beer," Martin's grandmother said, rather angrily.

Martin thought, "We must get the conversation back to this holiday." "I know," he said, suddenly picking up the newspaper, "we'll look at the weather reports in here."

So, while the two old people sat quietly, Martin and Jillian opened the newspaper on the table and told them about the places that had the most sun and the fewest wet days.

"Yes, there was least rain in Bournemouth yesterday."

"Windermere had a little sun, but Dover had less."

"There was a lot of wind there, too. But less wind at Bournemouth."

"And you'll have fewer young people and less noise at Bournemouth, grandfather."

"No, we shan't go to Bournemouth," Martin's grandmother said, suddenly.

"Oh," Martin thought, "she's going to say it takes less time and less money to go to Dover." And he began to think about taking them to Bournemouth in his car. They could travel more comfortably than in a train.

"No, we're going to a place that has more sunny days than Bournemouth," his grandfather said. "We're flying to Rome next Wednesday for two weeks."

Martin's mouth dropped open. He could think of nothing to say and nor could Jillian. They drove away more noisily than they arrived. "But I thought they had less money than that," Martin said, "and I was trying to decide if I could take them to Bournemouth on less petrol than Windermere."

"They think we haven't got much money," Martin's grandmother said, washing up the cups and saucers. "But we must have somewhere that has fewer cold days and showers than these English places."

"And I want to see more pretty girls," said grandfather very quietly, drying the cup she gave him.

"I was trying to tell them about Rome," grandmother said, "but they talk too much, those young people."

New words

a spoonful, to visit, a shower, wind, interesting, since.

Exercise 7

Read the story again and answer these questions.

Who was trying the most deliberately to make conversation?
In which of the three holiday places does it rain the most heavily?
In which does the sun shine the most often?
Can the old people travel more cheaply to Rome than to Dover?
Does Martin speak more loudly to Jillian or to his grandfather?

Does Jillian like more sugar or less than Martin's grandmother?
Did Martin and Jillian do more or less talking than the grandparents?
Did Martin think there are more or fewer noisy people in Bournemouth
    than in Dover?
Have Martin's grandparents more or less money than he knew?
Are there more or fewer cold summer days in Rome than in Windermere?

7

Exercise 8

Talk about your own country.

		the best the worst	weather	is — .
The One A Another	place that has	the least less only a little the most more	rain sun wind bad weather	
		the fewest fewer only a few the most more	showers cold days sunny days wet days	

Exercise 9

Peter Smith has written some more advertisements for new houses and his boss doesn't like them.

Peter wrote: "Other houses take more time to clean."
His boss wrote: "Our houses take less time to clean."
Read these five sentences Peter wrote, then write them again as Peter's boss wrote them.

Other houses are more trouble to clean.
People have more expenses with other houses.
There's always more noise in other houses.
Other houses have more stairs to climb.
Other houses give your wife more work.

Now here are five more sentences as Peter's boss wrote them. Write what you think Peter wrote about other houses.

There are more windows in each room in our houses.
Kitchens in our houses have more electric equipment.
People who live in our houses have more friends who want to visit them.
People who buy our houses have more money to spend on other things.
There are more trees in the gardens of our houses.

7

Exercise 10   Conversation practice

A | Which is the train to London that | goes the most slowly,
stops the most often, | please?

B | The 11.20 | takes the most time
stops at the most stations
is the slowest train

and that's why | it has the fewest passengers.
few people travel on it.

A   That's exactly what I want.

B | But you can get there more | quickly
comfortably

on the | 12.10 train.
train that leaves at 12.10.

A | Ah, but I'm travelling with |

my boss and I want to ask for more wages.
my girl friend and we can have more time together on the slower train.

Unit 8

Let's go
Let's not go

Let's dance, Jill.

No, let's not
dance, let's have
a drink.

Yes, let's both try
some wine.

Exercise 1

When Jillian, Philippa and Christina were getting ready for their party
they decided to do some things and not to do other things. Here are some
of their ideas.

We must buy lots of food and drink. We can ask Martin and the others.
We'll give the men beer. We won't give them any whisky.
We can dance. We'll share the expenses.
We won't spend a lot of money. Shall we get some new records?
We must not make too much noise. Shall we wear our best clothes?
It will be a good idea to stop at two o'clock. We won't send the men home
    before one.

Say again what they wanted to do, but this time use "let's" or "let's not".

8

Exercise 2

When Martin's grandparents were thinking about their holiday, they thought about the weather, how much the holiday was going to cost, and about travel. Write eight sentences.

Let's	go to find try	somewhere a place	that has a lot of rain. that has too much wind. that's easy to travel to. that's too expensive. that has less bad weather than Dover.
Let's not	go to try	anywhere a place	where we shall have the fewest wet days. where we can live as cheaply as we can. where Martin has been for a holiday.

I always go
I go every day

Philippa usually washes Jillian's hair.
She washes it on Friday evenings.
Jillian never washes Philippa's hair.
She goes to the hairdresser's once a week.

8

Exercise 3

How many true sentences can you make?

I	always usually sometimes never often	go home for lunch. have lunch at work. eat at the nearest restaurant. make my own lunch. meet my friends for lunch.

I	go home for lunch have lunch at work eat at the nearest restaurant make my own lunch meet my friends for lunch	every day. once or twice a week. when I can afford it. as often as I can. in autumn and winter.

Exercise 4

Tell your friends.

You	can will	always usually sometimes never often	see find	me at	home work the restaurant	at lunch-time.

The tennis enthusiast

The best tennis players in the world come to Wimbledon for two weeks every year. And those English tennis enthusiasts who can't get tickets to see the matches usually spend Wimbledon fortnight excitedly watching the players on the television or listening to them on the radio. Few people listen more keenly than Jillian. So when Martin asked her to go to the park one sunny day in Wimbledon fortnight last year, she decided that her transistor radio must go too. The big match she wanted to listen to was at half-past two.

76

8

"Let's sit in the rose garden," Martin said, carelessly taking her free hand, and thinking that he could look at the flowers when the tennis wasn't interesting. Old ladies often take their dogs through the rose garden and one looked rather unkindly at them as they sat down, still holding hands, at a few minutes to half-past two. Jillian turned to the transistor radio on the seat at her side.

"Let's switch it on, ready," she said. But as she put her hand out, the old lady suddenly turned round, accidentally pulling her dog across a bed of roses, and came up to their seat.

"Don't you know that those things are forbidden?" she shouted. "They won't let you play your horrible pop music in the park, I'm glad to say."

"But, but . . ." Jillian began, angrily standing up. And so did Martin as the little dog sat on his foot.

"I sometimes think that you young people never learn to read," the old lady said, and pointed angrily across the rose garden to a notice that said "No transistor radios".

"You do the least work and make the most noise as often as you can," she shouted, more loudly than before. "These gardens are for quiet people."

"Please let me speak," Jillian said, accidentally pushing the dog onto another rose bed, as she picked up her radio. "We were not going to play horrible pop music, as you call it. We want to listen to the tennis. But perhaps you think that's horrible too."

"You won't switch that awful thing on while I'm here," the old lady answered, deliberately sitting on their seat, and pushing the dog down at her side.

"The match starts at half-past two, Jill," Martin said, and pointed quietly to the park clock.

Jillian's eyes shone. "Nobody is going to stop me listening to this match," she said. "If they won't let me listen here, I'll go somewhere where I can. I'll be in the ladies' changing room at the tennis courts." And she walked quickly across the rose garden towards the tennis courts and switched on her radio noisily, as she went.

Martin smiled to himself as he watched her. "Meet me in the pub across the road when you're ready," he called. Then he laughed as the old lady stood up again and, excitedly pulling her dog behind her, began to go after Jillian.

Five minutes later Martin was sitting with his glass of beer outside the pub. As he slowly drank he could hear through the open window the big tennis match on a radio inside. He laughed to himself and went for some more beer.

He was still sitting outside the pub but not listening to the tennis, when Jillian came across the road, angrily carrying her transistor radio under her arm. "The match took less time than usual," Martin said. "Or won't they let you listen in there?"

8

"That woman." Jillian said. "I've never met anybody like her. I think she's mad. I'm sure she's mad."

"But haven't you been listening to the match?" Martin asked.

"She didn't let me hear a word," Jillian answered most unhappily. "I bought a tennis ticket and went into the ladies' changing room. But while I was trying to listen to the tennis that woman came and shouted and knocked on the window. Then she told the man who looks after the courts that I was inside and he got annoyed. Then when I opened the door that horrible little dog jumped up and knocked my radio onto the floor and now it won't work."

For a moment she was quiet but when she suddenly heard the radio from inside the pub she jumped to her feet. "That's the Wimbledon tennis!" she shouted. "And you have been listening to it all this time. What's happening?"

"I don't know," Martin answered, "I wasn't really listening."

As she spoke a man's voice from the radio said, "We are now leaving Wimbledon, because it's time for our programme for all dog lovers".

As Jillian dropped heavily back into her seat, Martin took the transistor radio from her carefully and said gently, "Let's not worry about the tennis. Let's have a drink."

But it was three o'clock and English pubs always shut at three.

New words

an enthusiast, world, a match, a fortnight, keenly, transistor, unkindly, accidentally, to let, to point, a pub, to call, mad, a lover.

Exercise 5

Look at the first picture in the story. Then put these broken sentences together correctly.

Martin and Jillian sat down	when Jillian put her hand on the radio.
An old lady looked unkindly at them	at a few minutes to half past two.
	when she suddenly turned round.
Martin held Jillian's hand	as he sat at her side.
The old lady stopped walking	as they sat down.
She pulled her dog across the rose bed	

Now do the same thing again with these sentences. Are they the same as the first five?

At a few minutes to half past two	he held her hand.
As Martin and Jillian sat down	Martin and Jillian sat down.
As Martin sat at Jillian's side	the old lady stopped walking.
When Jillian put her hand on the radio	she pulled her dog across the rose bed.
When the old lady suddenly turned round	an old lady looked unkindly at them.

Exercise 6

Now look at the second picture in the story. Write five sentences beginning with these words:

When Jillian came across the road — .
When Martin asked her about the tennis — .
While he was sitting outside the pub — .
When Jillian was in the ladies changing room — .
While the pub radio was going — .

Now write your sentences again, but this time finishing with the words you started with before.

Exercise 7

Read the story again and try to answer these questions.

How do you know that Jillian didn't get a ticket for Wimbledon?
How do you know that Jillian is keener on tennis than Martin?
Why do you think the old lady looked unkindly at them when they sat down?
How did the old lady know that radios were forbidden in the park?
Why did the old lady sit down on their seat?
Why did the old lady go after Jillian when she left the rose garden?
Why do you think Jillian bought a tennis ticket in the park?
Why didn't Jillian hear the pub radio when she first went to Martin?
Why didn't Martin know what was happening in the tennis match?
Why didn't Martin buy Jillian a drink?

8

Exercise 8

We can say: She didn't know that it was forbidden. *or* She didn't know it was forbidden.
They are both good sentences.

Now read the story again, then look at these pairs of sentences and try to remember which in each pair is from the story.

(a) She decided that her transistor radio must go too.
(b) She decided her transistor radio must go too.

(a) Martin thought that he could look at the flowers.
(b) Martin thought he could look at the flowers.

(a) Don't you know that those things are forbidden?
(b) Don't you know those things are forbidden?

(a) I sometimes think that you young people never learn to read.
(b) I sometimes think you young people never learn to read.

(a) Perhaps you think that that's horrible, too.
(b) Perhaps you think that's horrible, too.

(a) I think that she's mad. I'm sure that she's mad.
(b) I think she's mad. I'm sure she's mad.

(a) She told the man who looks after the courts that I was inside.
(b) She told the man who looks after the courts I was inside.

8

Exercise 9
Look at these three sentences.

"Let's sit here," Martin said, and took her free hand carelessly.
"Let's sit here," Martin said, and carelessly took her free hand.
"Let's sit here," Martin said, carelessly taking her free hand.

Now look carefully at these sentences from the story and decide if they are like the first, the second or the third sentence above. Then rewrite them like the other two.

The old lady suddenly turned round, accidentally pulling her dog across a bed of roses.

"But, but . . ." Jillian began, angrily standing up.

"You never learn to read," the old lady said, and pointed angrily across the rose garden.

"Please let me speak," Jillian said, accidentally pushing the dog.

"You won't switch it on," the old lady answered, deliberately sitting on their seat.

"The match starts at half past two," Martin said, and pointed quietly to the park clock.

She walked quickly across the rose garden and switched on her radio noisily as she went.

Jillian came across the road, angrily carrying her transistor radio.

Martin took the radio from her and said gently, "Let's have a drink."

Exercise 10   Conversation practice

A	Can Will	you let me	borrow use	your record-player, please?

8

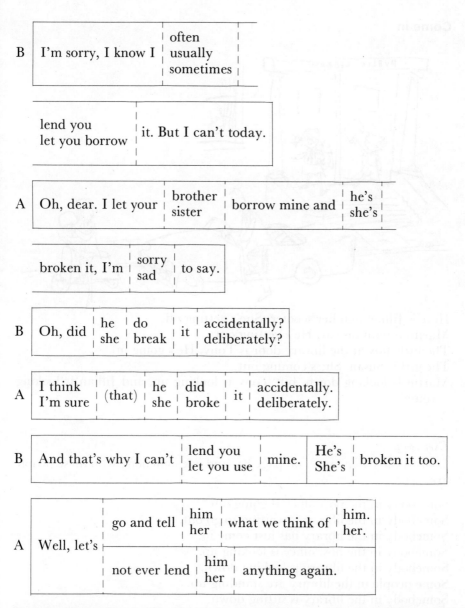

| B | I'm sorry, I know I | often
usually
sometimes |

| lend you
let you borrow | it. But I can't today. |

| A | Oh, dear. I let your | brother
sister | borrow mine and | he's
she's |

| broken it, I'm | sorry
sad | to say. |

| B | Oh, did | he
she | do
break | it | accidentally?
deliberately? |

| A | I think
I'm sure | (that) | he
she | did
broke | it | accidentally.
deliberately. |

| B | And that's why I can't | lend you
let you use | mine. | He's
She's | broken it too. |

| A | Well, let's | go and tell | him
her | what we think of | him.
her. |
| | | not ever lend | him
her | anything again. |

Practise again, but in the place of a record player talk about scissors or an alarm clock. This time the person who borrowed them has lost them.

Unit 9

Come in

Here is Jillian and her scooter. She's getting off.
Martin is with his car. He's getting out.
The little boy at the library door is Tony. He's going in.
The girl is Susan. She's coming out.
Martin is looking down, but Tony is looking up, and Jillian is looking
   round.

Exercise 1
Look at the two pictures on page 85, and ask somebody who these people
are.

Somebody in the post office is going out.
Somebody in the library is waiting to go out.
Somebody in the library has just come in.
Somebody in the post office is looking up.
Somebody in the library is looking down.
Some people in the library are standing up.
Somebody in the library is sitting down.
Somebody in the library won't turn round.
Somebody in the post office is walking away.

9

Exercise 2

Ask somebody:

When did you last
- get up too late?
- stand up for an hour?
- sit down for three hours?
- go out with your best friend?
- get home very late?
- go back to your old school?
- go away for a holiday?

Pick them up

In the picture at the beginning of this Unit, Jillian is holding her helmet.
Is she putting it on or taking it off? She's taking it off.
Tony is carrying a book. Is he taking it away or taking it back? He's
    taking it back.

Exercise 3

Look at the four pictures, then say something and ask something about
each one.

Jillian			football.	
Martin	has got a		skirt.	
Tony			transistor radio.	
Susan			dog.	

Is	he she	picking it up or putting it down? getting it out or putting it away? switching it on or switching it off? taking it away or bringing it back?

Exercise 4

Write true answers to these questions:

What have you thrown away this week?
What have you given away this month?
What clothes did you take off first last night?
What clothes did you put on last this morning?
What have you picked up today?
Who have you rung up this week?
On your next holiday what will you take away with you?
What will you bring back with you?
When you next go to the library, what book will you take back?
What book do you want to take out?

(Perhaps you will say, "I haven't thrown anything away this week", etc.)

Pick up everything you can see

Look back at the picture at the beginning of this Unit.

Jillian is taking something off.
She's taking off the helmet she wears on her scooter.
Susan is taking a book home.
She's taking home a book from the public library.
Tony is taking his book in.
He's taking in the book he's just finished.

9

Exercise 5

In the pictures in Exercise 3, Jillian is holding a skirt she has just bought, Martin has got Jillian's transistor radio, Tony is holding a football he borrowed from Tim, and Susan is holding a little black and white dog.

Now ask:

Who is	switching something on?
	taking something away?
	picking something up?
	getting something out?

Answer:

Jillian		switching something on.
Martin	is	taking something away.
Tony		picking something up.
Susan		getting something out.

Then ask:

What is	he	switching on?
	she	taking away?
		picking up?
		getting out?

And answer:

He's	getting out	a little black and white dog.
She's	switching on	a skirt she has just bought.
	picking up	Jillian's transistor radio.
	taking away	a football he borrowed from Tim.

Trouble with a case

Martin goes to his grandparents once or twice every month, and he decided to go round to see them when he had a free evening the week before they went away.

"Come in, Martin," his grandfather said. "I'm glad you've come round. Take your coat off and sit down near the fire for a minute. Let's

9

just see the end of this programme on the television. Your grandmother and I watch it every week at this time of night." So Martin sat in a comfortable chair, quietly waiting for the television detective to find out who the thief was.

Finally, his grandmother got up and switched the television off. Then, carefully putting on a hat she brought in from the hall, she said, "I'm sorry, Martin, but I must go and see a friend for a few minutes. I'll come back soon. But while I'm out, perhaps you'll help your grandfather to bring down the big blue case from the attic. We want it for the holiday and I don't really think he wants to get it down."

1

They watched her going by through the window. "She went into London three times last week," grandfather said, "to buy that hat. Now she's practising wearing it, ready for Italy. Let's go round to the pub for a drink."

"That's a good idea," Martin answered, "but let me give you a hand with the case. Tell me where it is and I'll get it out for you. It's in the attic isn't it?"

89

9

Grandfather pulled down the corners of his mouth. "That's the trouble. It's not there. You can go up and look, if you like, but you won't find it. I'm sure I haven't given it away and you don't throw away good cases like that, do you? I think, perhaps, I've lent it to somebody, but I can't remember. Your grandmother doesn't know, but she'll find out this week that we've lost our best case."

Martin laughed. "Don't worry. You can use mine. If I go home now I can bring it back in the car in half an hour. No, please, grandfather. You must let me lend you mine. It's the least I can do to help." And he went out quickly before the old man could say no.

When he got home, his father called, "What are you looking for, Martin? You're throwing your things about, aren't you?" And he came into Martin's room. But when Martin explained why he was lending his case to grandfather, his father suddenly looked guilty.

"Oh dear, I'm the one who borrowed his case. He lent it to me the year before last. I've been wanting to give him it back, but the longer I had it the harder it was. But, Martin, please take it back for me instead of yours and tell grandfather I'm very sorry."

When Martin walked into his grandparents' house with their lost case, grandfather laughed. "Of course," he said, "your father borrowed it; I remember now. But – er – let's not tell your grandmother I lent him it. Put it against the wall there."

Martin's grandmother came back from her friend's at that moment. "You two are looking guilty," she said, carefully taking off her new hat.

2

9

"But don't tell me. You didn't find the case, did you? You've given it away, or something, haven't you? I know you have. That's why you didn't want to go up to the attic when I asked you to bring it down. And that's why I asked you to go and get it out."

Grandfather smiled and pointed to the case standing against the wall. "You asked us to get it out," he said, "and there it is." Then he turned round and said, "Come on, young Martin, take me round to the pub and I'll buy you a drink."

They had not got to the pub before grandmother picked the case up and found a label that had on it Martin's father's name and address. She was still laughing when the two men came home.

New words

an attic, really, to go by, to give somebody a hand with something, instead of.

Exercise 6

Look at the two pictures in the story about the case, and decide which is the picture where these things are happening.

Martin has come round to his grandparents.
He has been back home.
He has put his coat on.
He has taken it off.
He is standing up.
He is sitting down.
He is looking round.
Grandfather is standing up.
He is sitting down.
Grandmother has switched the television off.
She is taking off the hat she has bought for the holidays.
She is putting her hat on.
She is going round to see her friend.
She has come back.
She is asking them to get out the big blue case.
She doesn't know they have got the case back.
She thinks grandfather has given away the big blue case.

9

Exercise 7

Martin went to his grandparents the week before they went away. Now make true sentences like that about yourself.

			grandparents
	went to see	my	uncle
	visited	our	cousins
I			friends
We			
My family			the park
My friend and I			an English pub
	went to		the cinema
			Wimbledon

			week.
	day		month.
	morning		year.
one	afternoon	last	spring.
	evening		summer.
	night		autumn.
			winter.

9

Exercise 8

Martin goes to his parents once or twice a month. Make true sentences like that about yourself.

I We My friend and I	(don't) go to	the library college the swimming pool work the theatre a football match	*(how often?)**

| * | once a
twice a | day.
week.
month. | | very
too | often. | | as | often
much
little | as | I
we | can. |

Exercise 9

Martin goes to his grandparents once or twice a month. Now make your sentences from Exercise 8 longer.

I We My friend and I	(don't) go to	the library college the swimming pool work the theatre a football match	*(how often?** when?***)*

| * | once a
twice a | day
week
month | | very
too | often | | as | often
much
little | as | I
we | can |

| ** | in | spring.
summer.
autumn.
winter. | | when | I feel like it.
the weather's fine.
I can afford it. |

9

Exercise 10   Conversation practice

MAN | Will you | come out with me / let me take you out | one evening next week?

GIRL | Well, I can't come on Monday because

I'm going out with my sister. / my sister's taking me out.

MAN | Well, | what about Tuesday or Thursday? / are Tuesday or Thursday any good?

GIRL | I | always / usually | clean the flat up / go round to my aunt's

on Tuesdays and Thursdays.

MAN | Then | can you come out on / are you doing anything on | Wednesday or Friday?

GIRL | A friend | often / sometimes | rings me up / comes round

every Wednesday and Friday at | eight / nine / ten | o'clock.

9

MAN	You're not very keen to	come out with me / let me take you out	are you?

GIRL	Oh yes. You decide the day and I'll put	something / somebody	off.

Unit 10

Point to them

Martin is talking about a picture. He's pointing to it.
Jillian's looking at it. She's thinking about it.
Martin is talking to Jillian. She's listening to him.

Exercise 1

Look at this picture again and ask:

Who is going into the library?
Who is getting out of the car?
Who is waiting for Martin?
Who is pointing to Martin?

Who is coming out of the library?
Who is getting off the scooter?
Who is looking at Martin?
Who is thinking about Martin?

10

What's he pointing to?

Exercise 2

Look at the picture of Jillian and Martin at the beginning of this Unit.

Martin is talking about something. What is he talking about?
Ask somebody five more questions like that.
Then look again at the picture in Exercise 1 and ask eight questions beginning "What is". (Use Exercise 1 to help you.)

Exercise 3

Look at this picture again and write five true sentences.

Martin's grandparents have been	thinking about	his grandparents.
His grandmother is	talking to	the television.
His grandfather is	looking at	her friend.
Martin is	pointing to	a big blue case.
They have been	talking about	Martin.

And now write five true sentences about this picture.

Martin's grandfather has been	walked into	
His grandmother has just	looking at	the big blue case.
His grandfather is	worrying about	the room.
Martin is	thinking about	his grandmother.
	listening to	

Exercise 4
Ask somebody:

Have you listened to anything interesting today?
Have you thought about anything interesting today?
Have you spoken to anybody interesting today?
Have you laughed at anything today?
Have you waited for anybody today?

Have you switched anything on today?
Have you knocked anybody down today?
Have you thrown anything away today?
Have you taken anybody home today?
Have you found anything out today?

10

The competition

Martin rang Jillian up one evening. "May I come round?" he asked.

"Of course," she said, "but on your way will you get me some shampoo? Ask for Shine. You pay for it and I'll give you the money when you get here. I want five packets."

"Five packets! Are you going to wash a horse?" he asked, and they both laughed at the idea.

"I'll explain when you come round," Jillian said mysteriously. "There's something we must think about," and she put the phone down.

When Martin walked into the living-room of Jillian's flat, she jumped up and held out a packet of shampoo. "But that's Shine," he said. "Why have I been going into half the shops in the country looking for it when you've got some already?" And he pulled out the five packets from his pocket. "I'm not going to take them all back," he said.

"Sit down quietly and let me explain," Jillian said, pointing to a comfortable chair. She held out her Shine packet again, turned it over, and pointed to the back. "Now listen to this, it's a competition, with a transistor television for the first prize." Then she read out: " 'Can you make up a good sentence for our television advertisements? Send us your sentence about girls who use Shine, together with six empty Shine packets.' And then it tells you about the prizes."

"Ah," said Martin, picking up another packet. "So that's what you were talking about on the phone. Well, let's try."

They worked for some time, making sentences up and writing them down on paper. Sometimes Martin didn't like what Jillian wrote down and she threw her paper away. Sometimes Jillian didn't like what Martin read out and he tore his paper up.

Finally, when they looked through the list of sentences they both liked, there were five. Martin read them out while Jillian looked at the paper over his shoulder. Martin read:

"Girls who ask for Shine know what is best.
Girls who look after their hair use Shine.
Girls who use Shine never worry about their hair.
Smart girls always look for Shine.
Men are always talking about girls who use Shine."

"Oh, I think our second sentence is the best," Jillian said, and so did Martin.

"Come on," he said, "let's send it tonight. I'll write our sentence out again properly while you empty the packets." So Jillian went into the kitchen and came back with a basin. She emptied the shampoo packets into it and Martin put them into an envelope with their sentence.

"I've got a stamp," he said. "I'll take the envelope round to the post-box now."

"And I'll get some coffee ready for when you come back," Jillian called as he went out.

He came in smiling a few minutes later. Two cups of coffee were ready on the table near the basin of shampoo. "Martin," Jillian said, as she switched the television on, "did you write my name and address down on that paper?"

He looked at her and sat down without a word. Jillian was still waiting for an answer when the television came on and an enthusiastic man's voice said, "Shine, the shampoo for you. Girls who look after their hair use Shine."

Neither of them spoke. But as Martin got up from his chair and switched the television off, Jillian picked the basin of shampoo up from the table, carried it into the bathroom and threw it away.

10

New words

a competition, to ring up, shampoo, mysteriously, to turn something over, a prize, to make up, to write something down, to tear something up, to write something out, properly, to get something ready, neither.

Exercise 5

Read the story again and try to answer these questions.

Who paid for the shampoo?
What did Jillian want Martin to help her think about?
Did Martin ask for Shine in half the shops in the country?
Why did they look at the back of the shampoo packet instead of the front?
Why did the Shine company want people to make up a sentence about girls who use Shine?
Why did Martin and Jillian tear up some of their pieces of paper?
Why did Jillian open the shampoo packets?
Do you think Martin wrote Jillian's name and address down with their sentence?
Why did the television man talk enthusiastically about Shine?
Why did Jillian throw the shampoo away?

Exercise 6

Let's have another competition, but this time you must write sentences advertising a new toothpaste, White Magic. Write ten sentences using these words.

to ask for, to look at, to look after, to look for, to pay for, to point to, to talk to, to talk about, to wait for, to worry about.

10

Exercise 7

Here are ten broken sentences from the story. Put them together, but when you write them down, say *how* you think they did these things.

There's something we must think		about.
She pointed		to the back.
That's what you were talking		about on the phone.
Finally they looked		through the list.
Jillian looked	*(how?)* *	at the paper over his shoulder.
Smart girls always look		for Shine.
Men are always talking		about girls who use Shine.
Jillian went		into the kitchen.
He looked		at her without a word.
Jillian was still waiting		for an answer.

* so mysteriously, slowly, keenly, most carefully, enthusiastically, uncomfortably, quietly, quickly, deliberately, with a shaking hand.

Exercise 8

Here are ten more sentences from the story. Put a word in to show *how** you think they did these things:

She put the phone down — .
Jillian jumped up — .
Martin pulled the five packets out — from his pocket.

10

She read out — "Can you make up a sentence?"
She threw her paper away — .
He tore his paper up — .
Martin read the sentences out — .
She switched the television on — .
He sat down — without a word.
The television came on — .

* quickly, rather angrily, sadly, carelessly, suddenly, excitedly, in a loud voice, carefully, heavily, unhappily.

Exercise 9
Think about Martin and Jillian and the competition and make up sentences like this.

Martin, Jillian, to ring up.   Answer: He rang her up.
Martin, a packet of Shine, to ask for.   Answer: He asked for it.

Now try these.

Martin and Jillian, the competition, to think about.
Jillian, a packet, to hold out.
Martin, many shops, to go into.
Jillian, a comfortable chair, to point to.
Jillian, the packet, to turn over.
Jillian, the words on the packet, to read out.
Martin, Jillian, to listen to.
Martin and Jillian, sentences, to make up.
Jillian, paper, to throw away.
Martin, paper, to tear up.
Martin, sentence, to read out.
Jillian, coffee, to get ready.
Jillian, television, to switch on.
Jillian, Martin's answer, to wait for.
Jillian, basin, to pick up.
Jillian, shampoo, to throw away.

10

Exercise 10

When Martin went round the shops looking for Shine, this is one conversation he had.

ASSISTANT   Good evening, sir. Can I help you?

MARTIN   Good evening. Do you sell Shine shampoo? I want five packets, please.

ASSISTANT   I'm sorry, we don't keep that one. We've got all these others on the counter. Try a packet of Sun Hat. I think it washes your hair best of all.

MARTIN   No thanks. I particularly wanted Shine. I'll leave it, thank you. Goodbye.

ASSISTANT   Goodbye.

In the last shop Martin went to, this was the conversation:

MARTIN   Good evening. Do you keep Shine shampoo?

ASSISTANT   Yes, of course, sir. Do you want it in a bottle or a packet?

MARTIN   May I have five packets, please?

ASSISTANT   Certainly. Here they are. That will be twenty-five pence, please.

MARTIN   Here you are. Thanks very much. Good evening.

ASSISTANT   Good evening.

Now practise shopping again. Ask for bottles of Sportsman ink, tins of Homecare paint, packets of Green Grass writing paper and envelopes, etc.

Unit 11

We come to the college to learn

Jillian is carrying some cups and saucers.
She's carrying them to take them into the kitchen.

Martin is taking his pipe out of his mouth.
He's taking it out to say something.

Sandy is sitting near the fire.
He's sitting there to get warm.

Jillian is looking round.
She's looking round to see where Martin is.

Martin is shouting.
He's shouting to stop her falling.

11

Exercise 1

Look at the two pictures on page 107 and put these broken sentences together.

The woman is opening her handbag	to take her book back.
The little boy has gone to the stamp counter	to help him walk.
The little girl is going to the children's library	to give to the library assistant.
The angry man is waiting at the counter	to read her book.
The old man uses a stick	to buy stamps.
The post office assistant has picked the phone up	to take a book out.
The woman in the library has sat down	to put something away.
The young man has bought some flowers	to talk to his wife.

Exercise 2

Answer these questions, using "to — ".

Why do people go to a library, a phone box, a launderette, a football match, a supermarket, a bowling alley, a pub, a swimming pool, a hospital, work?

Why do we use a toothbrush, a violin, binoculars, a spoon, a pen, a briefcase, a clock, an album, a tap, shampoo?

A book to read

In the picture at the beginning of this Unit:

Martin and Jillian had something to drink.
Martin hasn't got a chair to sit on.
The dog has found a warm place to sit.
Jillian has got a lot of cups and saucers to wash up.

11

1

2

11

Exercise 3
Ask somebody these questions and tell them to answer in full sentences.

When you get home tonight, will	you have there be	anything anybody	to talk to? to think about? to talk about? to remember? to worry about? to eat? to drink? to read?

The book is easy to read

In the picture at the beginning of this Unit:

Jillian's cups and saucers are difficult to carry. They are difficult cups and saucers to carry.
The table is low to sit at. It's a low table to sit at.

Exercise 4
Write true sentences.

Tennis Football Cricket	is isn't	easy expensive exciting			to play. to watch.
		an	easy expensive exciting	game	

11

			interesting easy difficult	
A	secretary's doctor's hairdresser's painter's photographer's policeman's	job	is isn't	an interesting one an easy one a difficult one	to do. to get.

The borrowers

Jillian had nothing to read in bed. "I've just finished a super book," she told Martin one Saturday night as he was taking her home, "and now I want something else to send me to sleep."

"I've got just what you want," Martin said, putting his arm round her waist. "I lent it to Peter last month. It's easy to read and not too heavy to hold when you are in bed. I'll go round to Peter's in the morning, to get it back." She was going to say something, but Martin kissed her to stop her talking. "No," he said, "I'm not going to tell you the title. Let it be a surprise. I'll bring it round in the morning about half past ten as soon as I've been to Peter's to get it. Goodnight."

So, early the next morning, Martin drove round to Peter and Liz Smith's house. "I've come to see if you've finished with that book I lent you," he said. "You know, *The Yellow Spider*. Jill wants something to read in bed."

"Oh, it's a marvellous story," Peter said. "I stayed up until two o'clock in the morning to finish it. I couldn't put it down. But – I'm sorry, Martin – I've lent it to Tom. He wanted something to stop him thinking about the examination he's just taken. And I thought your book was just the thing to do it. Oh, by the way, Liz borrowed Jillian's guitar last week. You'll be going to her flat to take her the book, so will you take the guitar back with you? It'll be easy to carry in your car."

Tom came to the door in his pyjamas. "I've just come down to make myself some breakfast," he said. "You haven't come to borrow anything, have you?"

Martin laughed.

11

"No, I've come to ask if you've finished with my book you borrowed from Peter," he said.

"Oh, *The Yellow Spider*, you mean," Tom said. "I say, let's talk somewhere else, it's cold here. Let's go into the kitchen, and then I can get something to eat. I thought it was a wonderful story," he said, switching the kettle on, "and it's very exciting to read. It's better than anything else I've read for a long time. But, you see, Mary borrowed it last month to pass the time on the train when she goes to work."

Martin put a hand over his eyes. "Oh," he said, weakly. "Oh, very well, I'll go round to her place to get it."

"A good idea, Martin," Tom said. "Oh, and while you've got the car, do you think you can take something back to Peter? I borrowed his ladder last week and it's easier for you to take it back in your car."

It was rather difficult for Martin to put Peter's ladder onto the car. Tom didn't come out because he was still wearing his pyjamas, and there was nobody else to give him a hand. But at last Martin drove away with the guitar and the ladder, hoping that Mary was not still in bed.

"Have you finished *The Yellow Spider*, Mary?" he asked, when she answered the door. "I went to get it back from Tom, but he says you've got it. Was it the right thing to pass the time on the train?"

Mary laughed as she showed him into the living room. "Yes," she said enthusiastically, "it's a super book. It's so hard to put it down. I went past my station twice last week because I was reading it in the train."

"Good," Martin said, looking at his watch. "May I have it back, please, to lend to Jill?"

"Oh, but I've lent it to Alison," Mary answered, opening her eyes wide, and before Martin could say anything else, she said, "I say, Martin, will you do something for me? Tom left his bicycle here last night when he came here to bring me home. Do you think you can take it back for him in your car? It's too heavy for me to ride."

It was half-past eleven when Martin stopped the car outside Alison's flat. He rang the bell and as he waited for her to come to the door he looked back sadly at the bicycle, the ladder and the guitar in the back of his car. "Please," he said, when Alison came, "have you got *The Yellow Spider*? I've been to Peter's and Tom's and Mary's to get it, but they've all lent it to somebody else. Er – no, I won't come in, Alison, thanks, I'm in a hurry."

But before Alison opened her mouth to speak, he knew the answer. "I lent it to Jillian last week," Alison said, "I didn't know it was yours." And when Martin looked behind Alison in the hall, he knew what she was going to ask him. There, against the wall, waiting for somebody to take it back, was Mary's sewing machine. Martin looked deliberately at Alison. "I'm in a hurry," he said, "I'm going to Tom's and Peter's to take their things back. And the car's not very easy to drive like that."

It was half-past twelve when Martin arrived at Jillian's flat. "I've been to four places to get that book and I've been to Tom's and Peter's again, to take things back. And now I find you've got the book I was looking for – *The Yellow Spider*," he told her angrily.

"Yes," Jillian said, "That's the title of that super book I was telling you about." She looked at him. "You know, you want a drink to make you feel better. Let's go round to the pub and I'll buy you one – if you can lend me fifty pence."

New words

super, else, sleep, a waist, a title, a surprise, marvellous, to stay up, until, to hope, pyjamas, a kettle, weakly, a watch, a sewing machine.

Exercise 5

Write answers to all these questions, using "to — ".

Why did Jillian want the book? Why did Tom? Why did Mary?
Why did Martin go back to Tom's and Peter's and Jillian's?
Why did Peter stay up until two o'clock in the morning?
Why did Tom go into the kitchen?
Why did Jillian and Martin go to the pub?
Why did Jillian borrow fifty pence from him?

11

Exercise 6

Look at the picture in the story.

Martin is in the picture. Is there anybody else there?
There's a ladder on the car. Is there anything else on it?
You can see two wheels on the bicycle. Can you see any wheels anywhere
  else?
Martin has come to see Alison. Has he been to visit anybody else?
Alison borrowed the sewing machine. Did she borrow anything else?
The car has been to Tom's and Mary's. Has it been anywhere else?
Martin is going to take the guitar back to Jillian. But first he is going to
  take something else to Peter. What?
Martin is going to Peter's but first he is going to go somewhere else.
  Where?
Martin is asking Alison for the book, but she has lent it to somebody else.
  Who?

Exercise 7

When Martin took Peter's ladder back, this is the conversation they had.

MARTIN   I've brought your ladder back, Peter.

PETER   That's very kind of you, Martin. I hope it wasn't too much
trouble to carry.

MARTIN   I'm always glad to help. Where shall we put it?

PETER   Let's take it into the garden.

Now make the conversation between Martin and Tom (about the
bicycle) and between Martin and Jillian (about the guitar). Then make
more conversations between yourself and your friends when you take
back things you have borrowed.

Exercise 8

Ask somebody:

What do you do Where do you go	when you want something	to eat? to drink? to do?	to read? to laugh at? to wear?

11

Who do you	go to look for	when you want somebody

to help you?
to talk to?
to dance with?
to take your troubles to?

Exercise 9

Do you remember the advertisements Peter Smith wrote? He has written some more, for electric kettles this time. But, as usual, his boss wants to change them.

Peter wrote: "Ours are easy kettles to use."
His boss wrote: "Our kettles are easy to use."

Here are some more of Peter's sentences. Write down what his boss wrote.

Ours are easy kettles to clean.
Ours are the cheapest kettles to buy.
Ours are super kettles to look at.
Ours are the quickest kettles to use.
Ours are the safest kettles to use.

Now here are the boss's sentences about pyjamas. Write out what you think Peter wrote first.

These pyjamas are easy to wash.
These pyjamas are cool to wear.
These pyjamas are comfortable to sleep in.
These pyjamas are smart to look at.
These pyjamas are light to wear.

11

Exercise 10   Conversation practice

A	I went to the cinema to see a	super marvellous wonderful	film	last night. the other night. yesterday.

B	What's the title? Which one?

A	It was	*Love in the Attic.* *The Saint.*	The actors It	is are	very exciting particularly good

to	watch. see.

B	Oh, I have been	wanting waiting hoping	to see that for a long time.

A	Well, if you've nothing	else better	to do	tonight tomorrow

come to see it with me.
let's go to see it together.

B	But	you've seen it once, haven't you? you said you went the other night, didn't you?

A	I	stood waited	in the queue for	half an hour twenty minutes	but I was too late to get in.

Unit 12

I know what to do

"Where do I go?"   Martin doesn't know where to go.
"What can I do?"   He doesn't know what to do.
"How can I get home?"   He doesn't know how to get home.
"Who can I ask?"   He doesn't know who to ask.

Exercise 1

Read these sentences. Three different people are speaking. One who is at a party, one going on holiday to England, and one starting a new job. Decide which person is speaking.

I don't know what is best to eat and drink.
I don't know where to stay.
I'm not sure what time to arrive.

I can't decide who to talk to.
I'm not sure where the lavatory is.
I don't know which restaurants to eat in.
I'm not sure when to stop work.
I don't know where to put my coat.
I can't decide what clothes to take.
I don't know how much money to take.
I'm not sure what I have to do.
I don't know when to leave.

Exercise 2

Look at the pictures on page 107 again. You are in the post office in England. Ask the woman with the handbag to help you.

Please	can will	you tell me	how	to find to use	a public telephone?
			where	to buy stamps? to post a letter?	

In the library, ask the library assistant to help you.

Please	can will	you tell me	how	to borrow a book? to use the library? to get a borrower's ticket?
			when	to bring books back? to ask for a new ticket?
			where	to find the children's library? to put the books I bring back?

Wherever I go, he's there

Everything Jillian does goes wrong.	Whatever she does goes wrong.
Everywhere Jillian goes, Martin goes.	Wherever Jillian goes, Martin goes.
Every time she reads in bed, she goes to sleep.	Whenever she reads in bed, she goes to sleep.
Anybody who talks to her laughs.	Whoever talks to her laughs.

Exercise 3

Peter has been writing advertisements again, but his boss changed his sentences so that they have in them "whatever", "wherever", "whenever", and "whoever". Read Peter's sentences, then write what you think his boss wrote.

Any time you want to know the time, look at a Tempo watch.
Everybody who wears a Tempo watch is always in good time.
Everywhere you go, people are wearing Tempo watches.
Anything we make goes for years.
Anybody who buys a Tempo watch knows what is best.
Wear a Tempo watch every time you want to look smart.
Take a Tempo watch with you everywhere you go.
A Tempo watch will make you early for everything you do.
People think about Tempo every time they look at a watch.
Buy a Tempo watch for anybody you love.

The ball pen

One Saturday afternoon Martin arrived in a great hurry at the flat Jillian shares with Philippa and Christina. "I don't know what to do or where to look," he said. "I've looked everywhere in our house and I've asked my parents and now I can't think where else to look or who else to ask," and he pushed his fingers through his hair and looked excitedly round the living-room.

"Martin," Jillian said, taking his arm, while Philippa and Christina looked at each other, "Martin, what is the matter? Just sit down and have

12

some coffee to make you feel better. But first tell us what you are looking for. Then we can decide what to do to help."

"I'm sorry," he said, taking the cup she gave him.

"Tell me when to stop," Philippa said as she filled it with coffee.

"That's fine, thanks," he answered. "Well, you know I came here last night to talk to Jill and we were all playing about with my green ball pen. Well, I can't find it." One of the girls, he thought, was playing a game with him, but he didn't know who to ask or how to get his pen back.

"We haven't got it," Philippa said, and Jillian said rather angrily, "A little thing like a ball pen is nothing to get excited about."

"You don't understand," Martin answered. "You see, old Aunt Myra bought me that pen three weeks ago. This morning I met her in the street and she said she's coming round to see us tomorrow. And you know what she's like. Whenever she gives somebody a present, she always wants to see it later. So, please, whoever has got it, may I have it back."

The three girls looked at each other again, not knowing what to say. "Oh, come on, let's look for it," Christina said, "but if it isn't in this room I don't know where else to look."

"Can't you buy another one exactly the same?" Philippa asked, on her knees under the table.

"Perhaps," Martin answered, as he looked on the bookshelf, "but there are so many different ball pens and so many shops, I don't know which to go to."

Soon there was nowhere else to look, and Martin decided to go. "I'm sorry to be a nuisance," he said as he went out, "but I really don't know what to do now."

The next afternoon, Martin was at home and happy because he had a green ball pen in his pocket, when the door bell rang. Thinking it was Aunt Myra, he put the pen in the middle of the living-room table and went to answer the door. It was Jillian. "Here," she said, and held out another green ball pen, exactly like Martin's. "We didn't know how to get you another one, but Christina rang up her brother Sidney and asked him where to buy them. And he went round to the old lady next door and she told him which shop to try. So I've bought you one, and here it is."

At that moment she saw the second pen on the table. "Oh, and after all our trouble, you've found yours. Where was it?"

"No," Martin said, "this isn't the one I lost. When I left you yesterday I didn't know where to get another, so I went round five or six shops, but wherever I went they hadn't any ball pens this colour. I couldn't think of anywhere else to try, but when I went to buy some tobacco for the weekend, I saw a box of these on the counter."

"So now you've got two and you don't know which to show Aunt Myra," Jillian said laughing.

Then, before Martin could think what to do with the two green ball pens in his left hand, his mother came into the room with Aunt Myra. Martin quickly put his left hand behind his back and held out his right to shake hands with Aunt Myra. But the old lady stood still, opened her bag and said, "You're getting careless, young Martin. You dropped this in the street yesterday when we met." And she gave him the green pen he lost. "Whoever marries you," she said, looking at Jillian, "will have to teach you how to look after your presents."

Jillian tried not to smile, but Aunt Myra suddenly said, "Why do you young people always laugh at whatever I say?" And as Martin turned towards Jillian the old lady saw the other pens he was holding. "Oh, so you've got all those ball pens! If you don't know what to do with them, you can give me one." She turned to Martin's mother. "That's lucky," she said. "That nice young man Sidney who lives next door to me was asking where to buy them only last night. Thank you, Martin, he can have one of yours. And I hope," she said, shaking a finger at him, "he knows how to look after it better than you do."

New words

to play about, ago, a knee, a weekend, to have to, lucky.

Exercise 4

Write answers to these questions.

Why did Martin go to Jillian's flat?
Why did he push his fingers through his hair?
Why was Jillian rather angry?
Why was Martin so keen to get his pen back?
Why did Martin put the new pen in the middle of the table when he thought Aunt Myra was coming?
Why did Christina ring Sidney up?
Who lives next door to Sidney?
Why was it difficult to buy another pen exactly the same as Martin's?
Why did the old lady look at Jillian?
What will happen when Aunt Myra takes the pen to Sidney?

Exercise 5

Here is the conversation between Sidney and Aunt Myra.

SIDNEY   My sister wants to know where to go to buy a green ball pen. Can you tell her?

AUNT MYRA   Why yes. I bought one like that three weeks ago for my favourite nephew. Now let me think. I was looking for somewhere to buy a dictionary. Yes, I know. I got it in the bookshop in the High Street.

SIDNEY   That's fine. Now I can ring my sister up and tell her where to find one. Thanks very much.

AUNT MYRA   Not at all.

Now make up conversations between you and a friend asking how to buy a train timetable, an electric switch and an egg cup.

Exercise 6

Write ten true sentences. (I have to go = I must go.)

When I	go to work went to school go away on holiday	I	have had shall have	to

get up leave the house	at — o'clock.

Whenever I stay When I stayed Next year when I stay	in a hotel, I	don't didn't shan't

have to	make my own bed. carry my own case. take my own soap.

12

Exercise 7

A friend who is going to England is not sure what to do. He asks you these questions.

Where shall I stay?
How do you get from London to Manchester?
Where do you buy toothpaste?
What shall I bring back for you?
Who can I ask for help, if I get lost?
When do people have lunch?
What do I say when people say "Thank you"?
Where do I find a taxi?
How much do you give the driver?
How can I get a job?

Now put your friend's questions in another way.

He She	doesn't know wants to know wants to find out asked me	where how what who when how much	to — , etc.

Can you answer these questions?

Exercise 8
Tell somebody:

I last went to	a park a birthday party a secondhand shop a hospital a theatre	—	days weeks months years	ago.

Then ask them when they last went. Say: What about you?

12

Now tell them:

		a helicopter a football match an English one pound note a sewing machine an encyclopaedia		days weeks months years	
I first	saw used		—		ago.

What about you?

Exercise 9

Look at this picture once again.
These sentences are what the people are thinking. Who do you thin
thinking:

Wherever they go they make too much noise.
Whenever I hold her hand somebody else arrives.

Whatever we do she'll say it is wrong.
Whenever I come in here I bring my dog.
I'm going to listen however I can.
Whoever pulls a dog about like that isn't very kind.
Whenever the tennis is on he takes me out.
Whoever comes in here must be quiet.
Wherever we go she's still thinking about tennis.
I will follow her wherever she goes.

Exercise 10   Conversation practice

A	Do you know	how to put a watch together? what to do with a broken watch?

B	Ask John.	Whatever Whenever anything	is	wrong broken	he	always thinks he

	knows	what to do. how to put it right.

A	Yes,	whatever whenever	I ask him, he usually	tells me knows	how to mend things. who can help.

B	He's rather a big head. I never listen to	what he says. his ideas.

A	But he told me	to ask you you know	how to mend what to do with

	this watch, because it's yours.

Unit 13

When I arrived, the film had started

Here is a photograph of Martin when he was twelve. When somebody took this photograph, Martin had just got his first long trousers. Before this he had always worn short trousers. But here his parents had just bought him his first long pair.

1 *My first long trousers. Age 12.*

Exercise 1

Here are five more old photographs from Martin's album.

Ask somebody:

When Martin was	8 17 20 21 22	had he	learnt how to swim? learnt how to drive a car? met Jillian? got his dog, Sandy? bought his car? started smoking a pipe?

Answer: Yes, he had. No, he hadn't. *or* I don't know.

Exercise 2

Look again at the six photographs of Martin. Ask somebody:

What had Martin just done? Who or what had he got with him?

Answer: When somebody took this photograph, {Martin had just —.
Martin had got —.

124

13

2 *At the swimming pool. Age 8.*

3 *After my first driving lesson. Age 17.*

4 *An early walk with Jill. Age 20.*

5 *My first car. Age 21.*

6 *In the mountains. Age 21.*

Exercise 3

Think about yourself, and your friends, and answer these questions.

Have Has	you he she	learnt how to	swim? drive a car? ride a horse? write? use a camera?

Had	you he she	learnt how to	swim drive a car ride a horse write use a camera	when	you were	1? 4? 8?
					he she was	10? 16?

The car he had bought

Exercise 4

Look at the six photographs of Martin in Exercise 1 and write out these sentences correctly.

In the first photo he was wearing	the mountain he had climbed.
In the second photo he was wearing	a plastic ring somebody had given him.
In the third photo he was looking at	the car window he had broken.
In the third photo he was worrying about	the dog he had bought.
In the fourth photo he was walking with	the long trousers he had just got.
In the fourth photo he was thinking about.	the car he had bought.
In the fifth photo he was standing near	the tree he had hit.
In the sixth photo he was sitting on	the pipe he had brought with him.
In the sixth photo he was smoking	a girl he had just met.
In the sixth photo he was looking at	the girl he had brought with him.

13

How Martin met Jillian

"Martin, look what I've found," Jillian called, holding up an old notebook she had taken from a drawer. Martin had seen it before, but pretended he hadn't. He remembered that Jillian had just bought the notebook when they first met. She had filled it with shorthand, but instead of throwing it away like all her other old notebooks, she had carefully kept it. And whenever Jillian had found it again she had started to get sentimental. "Or perhaps," Martin thought, "she gets it out whenever she wants to be sentimental." So he didn't show much interest in the shorthand notebook.

But Jillian knew he had seen it before. "You remember the day we first met, Martin," she said. "This is the notebook I had just bought." Martin let her talk. "I had put my name down for a shorthand examination and my teacher had told me to get some practice. So I went and sat in that coffee bar and wrote down whatever I heard."

Martin smiled as he thought about it. He and his boss had not noticed the young lady who was writing at the next table to theirs in the coffee bar. But when they had nearly finished their conversation, Martin's boss put a hand out and said quietly, "I'm sure that girl has been writing down everything we've been saying. You can read shorthand, Martin, can't you? Find out what she's written. Perhaps she's a reporter. We don't want everything we've been saying to go into the newspaper."

Martin smiled again to himself, remembering how his boss had gone back to the office, leaving him to find out what this girl had written. He had never spoken to her before; he had never seen her before.

Then he heard Jillian's voice. "You had never seen me before, had you, Martin?" she laughed. "Do you remember, when your boss had gone, you weren't sure how to start a conversation. So you asked me to have another cup of coffee. I think you had been watching me." A far-away expression came into her eyes. "Isn't it marvellous, Martin? Somebody looks across a coffee bar at somebody else and – zing – he falls in love. Just like that."

Martin laughed weakly. "She doesn't know," he thought to himself. "She thinks I went to talk to her because I had fallen in love with her. She doesn't know my boss had told me to find out what she'd written in her notebook."

But Jillian began talking again. "And then you pretended you could

13

read my shorthand. But when you saw it, you couldn't read what I had written."

"That's not true," Martin said. "You had written a lot about me. I can tell you now, but I couldn't then. It said, 'I like his eyes. Isn't he super? He's just like that marvellous man on the television. Oh, the older man has just called him Martin.' You see?" Martin said, looking at Jillian, "When I had seen all those nice things you were thinking, I couldn't read them out to you."

Now Jillian began to laugh. "And you thought I had fallen in love with you. Oh, Martin. I told you I was practising shorthand. All that about your eyes was a conversation I had written down from two silly girls at the next table to you. I'm sorry. I don't think I had looked at you more than once. But when you came up to me after your boss had gone, I knew . . ."

Suddenly Martin burst out laughing. "Jill, stop. I must tell you," he said. "I didn't come to talk to you because I had fallen in love with you. My boss told me to look at what you had put down in your notebook, because he thought you had written down our conversation. He thought you were a reporter."

They both laughed, looking into each other's eyes. Then, as Martin took Jillian in his arms and kissed her, he pushed the old shorthand notebook off the table into the fire. "We must think about getting married," he said softly in Jillian's ear. She looked at him. And when he saw the happy expression in her eye, he knew why she had suddenly found her shorthand notebook again.

New words

to hold up, a notebook, to pretend, sentimental, interest, a bar, to notice, a reporter, far-away, an expression, to burst out, to get married.

Exercise 5

Read the story again, then answer these questions. Write full sentences for your answers.

When Martin went into the coffee bar, had Jillian started writing?
When his boss noticed Jillian, had he finished his conversation with Martin?

When the boss left the coffee bar, had Martin spoken to Jillian?

When Martin bought Jillian a cup of coffee, had she had one already?

When Martin looked up from the shorthand book, had he understood what Jillian had written?

Did Martin speak to Jillian because he had fallen in love with her?

Did Jillian write nice things about Martin because she had thought them?

Did Jillian sit in the coffee bar because her teacher had told her to practise shorthand?

Did Martin buy Jillian a cup of coffee because he hadn't thought of anything else to say?

Did Jillian show Martin the old notebook because she had felt sentimental?

Exercise 6

A plane left London Airport at 12 o'clock. It flew exactly 500 miles an hour. Now ask ten questions.

How	many miles far	had it	flown travelled gone	at	1 2 3 4 5	o'clock?

What	time was it was the time	when it had	flown travelled gone	250 750 1,250 1,750 100	miles?

13

Exercise 7

Look at the two pictures on page 131.

In the first picture:

The lady with the handbag has bought something. Had she bought it at two o'clock?

The assistant at the stamp counter has sat down. Had she sat down at two o'clock?

The little boy's mother has written a letter. Had she written it on May 7th?

The man using the telephone has started to write. Had he started at half past two?

The old man with the stick has asked for a stamp. Had he asked for it at half past two?

In the second picture:

The little girl has finished her book. Had she finished it on October 24th?

The young man has bought some flowers. Had he bought them at a quarter past ten?

The library assistant has worked for a year. Had she worked here a long time last December?

The angry man has decided which book to read. Had he decided at twenty five minutes past ten?

The woman on the chair has found a good book. Had she found it on November 23rd?

Exercise 8

Finish these sentences by using either "had" or "hadn't".

Martin — seen Jillian before they met in the coffee bar.

He — noticed her when he first went in.

He — learned shorthand.

Jillian — decided to take a shorthand examination before she met Martin.

13

1

2

131

She — written down Martin's conversation with his boss.
Martin's boss — been in his office before he went into the coffee bar.
Martin — fallen in love with Jill when he first spoke to her.
Jill — used her shorthand notebook a lot before she went to practise in the coffee bar.
When she showed the old book to Martin, she — found it deliberately.
When Martin talked about getting married, Jill — thought about it.

Exercise 9
Think about yourself.

Have you spoken to anybody today you had never spoken to before?
Have you met anybody this week you had not met before?
Have you written to anybody this year who had never written to you?
Have you been anywhere this week you had never been to before?
Have you eaten anything today you had never eaten before?
The last time you went to the cinema, had you heard anything about the film?
The last time you read a book, had anybody told you to try it?
The last time you ate in a restaurant, had you eaten there before?
The last time you were ill, had you eaten or drunk too much?
The last time you smiled at anybody, had they smiled at you first?

Exercise 10   Conversation practice

A Why did you go home before the party had finished?
B I thought I had forgotten to switch my electric fire off.
A What had happened when you got home?
B My brother had switched it off for me.
A Then why didn't you come back to the party?
B Sh! I had left the fire on deliberately because I didn't want to stay at the party.

Now make a new conversation. Instead of leaving a party, B left a cinema before the film had finished, and he pretended he had forgotten to switch a shower tap off.

Make another conversation. A woman went home from a restaurant before she had finished her lunch. She had forgotten to take a cake out of the oven. When she got home she found she had forgotten to switch the oven on.

And another one. A man went away from a football match because he thought he had left his glasses in the car park. When he got to his car they weren't there. They had been in his pocket all the time. But he was so annoyed because he had been silly that he accidentally dropped them and broke them. So he couldn't go back to the football match.

Unit 14

I had been waiting

Susan is reading. She was reading
when Martin looked round the door.
But before he came in, she had been
eating a banana.

Exercise 1

Martin's grandfather started work when he was fifteen. Ask somebody:

How long had he been working when he was 20? 25? 32? 40? 45? 53?
Martin's grandmother was twenty when she got married.
How long had she been looking after her own house when she was 25?
  36? 41? 54? 59? 62?

Exercise 2

Look at the picture of cars in the car park again on page 61.

At a quarter past two how long had each car been standing there?
Which car had been standing there the longest and which the shortest
  time?
At a quarter past two which cars had been waiting for more than an hour?
Which had been waiting for less than half an hour?
The first car is Peter's. He came for his car at 4.30. How long had he been
  sitting in the cinema?
The second car is Margaret's. She came back at 2.40. How long had she
  been eating in the restaurant?
The third car is Jillian's mother's. She came back at 3.30. How long had
  she been shopping?

Exercise 3

Look at the six photographs of Martin again.

14

1 *My first long trousers. Age 12.*

2 *At the swimming pool. Age 8.*

3 *After my first driving lesson. Age 17.*

4 *An early walk with Jill. Age 20.*

5 *My first car. Age 21.*

6 *In the mountains. Age 21.*

Before each photograph he had been doing things. Write out six correct sentences.

Before somebody took the	first second third fourth fifth sixth	photograph, Martin had been

buying Jill some flowers.
trying to swim.
climbing with Jillian.
having a driving lesson.
fishing.
taking Jillian out in the car.

Exercise 4
Look at these sentences.

Jill first went climbing when she was twenty-one.
She had never gone climbing before.

Now talk about yourself and make pairs of true sentences like that. Tell somebody how old you were when you first went to a cinema, a theatre, a concert, a party, a dance.

Now do the same thing with the first time you saw somebody, met somebody, spoke to somebody; and the first time you bought something, lost and found something, made or broke something.

The engagement ring

Martin looked quickly up the street and down to make sure that nobody was watching him, then he turned round, pushed open the door of the jeweller's shop and walked smartly up to the man who was standing behind the counter.

He had been passing this shop for many months, because it was near Jillian's flat. But he had only been looking in the window for a few days. Once he and Jillian had started to talk about getting married, he knew he ought to buy her an engagement ring. So he had been window-shopping in all the jewellers' shops he could find. But since he had seen one particular ring in the shop nearest Jillian's flat, he had not been thinking seriously about any others. This, Martin decided, was the ring for Jillian. And so he had gone into the shop to see it more closely.

14

"I've been looking at a lot of rings lately," he told the assistant, "but I'm sure this is the one for my young lady. Yes, she ought to like it," he said, looking at the price ticket. The man behind the counter smiled.

"I'm sure she will, sir. But if the size isn't right, or if she wants to change it, please bring it back."

At half past ten that night Martin found himself walking in the rain towards Jillian's flat. At his side were Jillian and Philippa, talking noisily. But Martin was silent. He had turned the collar of his raincoat up and had pushed his hands deep into his pockets. In his right hand was a little square box; in the box was the engagement ring.

Why, he thought, had things gone wrong, as usual? He had been looking forward to this evening. Since he had bought the ring he had been thinking only about the best time and the best place to put it gently on Jillian's finger. He had been making up romantic things to say. He had been thinking about romantic places to say them. But Jillian had asked to go out for a walk. There was something she had been wanting to show him, she said. Then it had started to rain and they had met Philippa. So now they were all going home.

Suddenly Jillian said, "We'll see you at the flat, Philippa. This way Martin. This is what I've been wanting to show you." And as Philippa left them, Jillian stopped in front of the jeweller's shop where Martin had bought the ring earlier in the day. Then, for a moment, she was silent. "It's gone," she said in a small voice. "Martin, I've been looking at engagement rings since the other day. And I've been thinking particularly about one I saw in this window. But it's gone." She turned away from him as she burst out crying. "I'm sorry, Martin," she said, "lend me your handkerchief, please."

Martin brought his hand out of his raincoat pocket. "Is this what you've been looking at?" he asked, opening the little square box. The ring shone in the rain.

"We had both been looking in the same shop," he said.

"We'd both been looking at the same ring," she answered.

"And I've been carrying it about in my pocket since this afternoon," Martin said, as he put it on her finger, "waiting for the right moment to give you it."

"You ought to cry more often," he said, when he had kissed her. "It makes you look pretty."

She laughed. "I promise I'll cry whenever you buy me a ring." And they both laughed.

14

As they walked slowly through the rain towards the flat, Martin said, "Do you think we ought to ring up your parents and mine to tell them about our engagement?"

"Ring them up?" Jillian said. "Let's go up on the roof and shout."

New words

an engagement, a jeweller, smartly, ought, particular, seriously, closely, a price, silent, deep, square, to look forward, romantic, a walk, a handkerchief, to promise.

Exercise 5

Write answers to these questions.

How long had Martin and Jillian been thinking seriously about getting married?

How long had Martin and Jillian been passing the jeweller's shop?

How long had they been looking at engagement rings?

How long had Martin been carrying the ring about in his pocket before he gave it to Jillian?

Why had Martin been looking forward to that particular evening?

Why had they been going for a walk?

What had Jillian been wanting to show Martin?

Why had she been wanting Martin to see it?

When Jillian asked for Martin's handkerchief, what had she been doing?

When they got to Jillian's flat, how long had she been wearing her ring?

Exercise 6

Martin's friend, Tom, is a newspaper reporter. When he had been in his job for only one week, his boss told him to write a report about two ships. The news had just arrived to say that the two ships had gone down. The boss wrote a few words on a piece of paper and gave it to Tom with an old report to help him. Here is the old newspaper report and the paper Tom's boss gave him. When you have read them both, write Tom's report for him.

Last night there was an accident in the mouth of the Thames, when two ships went down. The smaller ship, the *White Rose*, had been going from London to Rotterdam. The other, the *Lady of Lisbon*, had been coming to London from Japan. The *White Rose* had been carrying bicycles and six passengers. The bigger ship had been bringing electrical equipment. Both ships had been travelling slowly and showing the usual lights. Before they went down, a third ship took all the people off, and later brought them to London.

From London to Singapore,
carrying cars,
going slowly.

From Abadan to London,
carrying oil, going quickly,
doing this for 5 years.

Both showing usual lights, all men safe.

Exercise 7
Ask somebody:

What time ought you to go to bed? What time do you go?
How much money ought you to spend? How much do you spend?
How many English books ought you to read a year? How many do you read?
What time ought you to arrive at work? What time do you arrive?
How slowly ought cars to go in towns? How slowly do they go?
How old ought girls to be before they get married? How old are they, sometimes?
What ought the police to do when an accident happens? Do they always do it?
Ought little boys to smoke cigarettes? Do they sometimes?
How often ought you to clean your teeth? Do you?
How often ought you to clean your shoes? Do you?

14

Exercise 8

Here is the conversation Jillian had with her friend Liz when she rang up to tell her about her engagement.

JILLIAN There's something I've been waiting to tell you, Liz.

LIZ Oh, is it good news, or bad?

JILLIAN Oh, it's good. Martin and I have decided to get married.

LIZ Oh, yes, that's wonderful. Congratulations. I hope you'll both be very happy.

JILLIAN Thank you. I'm sure we shall.

Now make up another conversation between yourself and a friend when you have just passed an examination. Then try again for when you have just got a much better job. And a third conversation telling somebody that you have won the first prize in a competition.

Exercise 9

Find somebody who has changed jobs or houses and ask:

Where did you	work live	before you changed	jobs? houses?

How long have you been	working living	in this	job? house?

How long had you been	working living	in the other	job? house?

Find somebody who was going to a different class before they started English. Ask:

What	did you study class did you go to	before you started	this class? English?

140

14

| How long have you been | studying English? |
| | coming to this class? |

| How long had you been | going to the other class? |
| | studying the other subject? |

Find somebody who has just bought their first car or scooter. Ask:

| How did you travel | before you bought your new | car? |
| What did you use | | scooter? |

| How long have you been | using | this | car? |
| | driving | | scooter? |

How long had you been	riding	a scooter?
	using	a bicycle?
		a horse?
	travelling	by train?
		by bus?
		on foot?

Exercise 10   Conversation practice

| A | Do you still want to go to | England | for your holidays? |
| | | America | |

| B | No, | I don't want to any more. |
| | | I've changed my mind. |

14

| A | But | you hadn't changed your mind the last time we met.
you were always talking about going there.
you have always wanted to go there. |

| B | I know.
That's true. | I had | been hoping
always wanted | to go until last | month.
week. |

| A | What | happened last | month?
week? |
| | | made you change your mind? |

| B | I | read
found out
heard | that | English
American |
| | Somebody told me | | | |

| beds are the most uncomfortable
hotels are the most expensive
women are the ugliest
food is the most uninteresting
weather is the worst | in the world. |

| A | Oh, I have always | thought
heard
understood | that | it isn't
they aren't | too bad. |

Unit 15

He said, "I am working"
He said he was working

1
Tony carrying
a violin

2
Martin getting
a raincoat

3
Tim mending
a ship

4
Jillian looking at
a ring

5
Peter and Liz
painting a house

Exercise 1

Look at the five people in the pictures above. Pretend you asked them all,
"What's that?"
Tony said, "It's a violin." Tony said it was a violin.
Now say two sentences like that for each of the others.

15

Pretend you asked them all, "What are you doing to it?"
Tony said, "I'm carrying it." Tony said he was carrying it.
Say two sentences like that for each of the others.

Pretend you asked them all another question – "Whose is it?"
Tony said, "It's my violin." Tony said it was his violin.
Say two more sentences like that for each of the others.

And pretend you asked them all, "What are you doing?"
Tony said, "I'm carrying my violin." Tony said he was carrying his violin.
Say two more sentences like that for each of the others.

He asked, "What are they doing?"
He asked what they were doing

Exercise 2

How many sentences can you make?

I	wanted to know asked found out know, now,	what	Tony was carrying.
		whose	violin raincoat ship ring house	Martin was getting. Tim was mending. Jillian was looking at. Peter and Liz were painting.

He said, "I understand"
He said he understood

I asked, "Do you understand?"
I asked if he understood

Do you smoke cigarettes?

Do you like pop music?

Does Martin like pop music?

No, I don't smoke.

Yes, I like it very much.

Yes, he likes it too.

Tom asked Jillian if she smoked cigarettes. She said she didn't smoke.
He asked her if she liked pop music. She told him she liked it very much.
He asked her if Martin liked pop music. She answered that he liked it, too.

Exercise 3
Look back at the five people at the beginning of this Unit.

Tony was thinking, "I don't like my violin lesson. I hope my teacher is ill."
Martin was telling himself, "My coat looks the dirtiest. I can't afford a new one."
Tim was saying, "Tony doesn't know it's broken. I know what to do."
Jillian was thinking, "I love Martin. My ring shines like fire."
Peter and Liz were saying, "We don't want to do any more. There's paint on both our faces."

Now put these broken sentences together correctly.

Tony was telling himself
Martin was thinking
Tim was telling himself
Jillian was saying to herself
Peter and Liz were telling themselves
Tony was saying to himself
Martin was saying to himself
Tim was saying
Jillian was telling herself
Peter and Liz were saying

Tony didn't know it was broken.
her ring shone like fire.
he didn't like his violin lesson.
there was paint on both their faces.
his coat looked the dirtiest.

she loved Martin.
he hoped his teacher was ill.
they didn't want to do any more.
he knew what to do.
he couldn't afford a new coat.

Exercise 4
Write down the exact words you used the last time you did these things.

— asked somebody {
  what the time was.
  what their address was.
  what size their shoes were.

— asked somebody {
  if they liked dancing.
  if they lived far away.
  if they remembered you.

— told somebody {
  you knew their friend.
  you liked their hair.
  they made you feel happy.

— told yourself {
  you were being silly.
  you were feeling faint.
  you couldn't afford to spend any more.

He said, "I have done it"
He said he had done it

The policeman said, "You have broken the law. You have been going
  too quickly."
The policeman told Tom he had broken the law. He had been going too
  quickly.
The policeman asked, "Have you broken anything? Have you been
  drinking?"
The policeman asked Tom if he had broken anything and if he had been
  drinking.

15

Exercise 5
Look at the six old photographs again.

1
*My first long
trousers. Age 12.*

2
*At the swimming
pool. Age 8.*

3
*After my first driving
lesson. Age 17.*

4
*An early walk
with Jill. Age 20.*

5
*My first car.
Age 21.*

6
*In the mountains.
Age 21.*

Martin is talking in each picture.

1 I've just put my new long trousers on.
   I've been fishing.

2 I've just come out from my lesson.
   I haven't been doing very well.

3 My teacher has just decided to change his job.
   I haven't been learning very long.

15

4 I've bought Jill some flowers.
We haven't been going out together very long.

5 I've only had my car a week.
We've just been having a wonderful ride.

6 We've just arrived at the top.
Jillian has been taking a lot of photographs of me.

Now write down what Martin was telling us in each photograph. Like
this: Martin was saying he had just put his new long trousers on. He said
he had just been fishing.

Somewhere to live

Martin sat down heavily in one of Jillian's armchairs and sighed. Since
they had decided to get married, they had both been looking for somewhere to live. At first they thought it was going to be easy to find a flat, but
they soon found out it was more expensive and more difficult than they
had thought.

"How did you get on, Jill?" Martin asked. She came and sat on the
arm of his chair.

Well, I phoned the house agent I told you about. I said we were going
to get married soon and we wanted a flat. He asked if we wanted a
ground floor flat and I told him it didn't matter. He wanted to know if
we wanted one bedroom or two, and I said one was enough. Then he
said he hadn't got any small flats at the moment. He said he had been
looking for a one-bedroom flat for somebody else for five weeks and he
couldn't find one. But I've got his phone number and I promised to ring
him up again during the week."

"Mm," said Martin. "That doesn't look very hopeful, does it? Well,
you remember I promised to go to the house agent's in the High Street.
They have had a list of flats in their window for as long as I can remember.
So I thought they ought to be able to help us. The assistant asked where
we wanted to live, and I said it didn't really matter. Then he asked how

much rent we could afford, so I told him we didn't want a big expensive flat. And he wanted to know if we were in a hurry."

They both laughed and Jillian said, "Yes, we haven't thought what we shall do if we find a flat tomorrow. What did you tell him?"

"I said we'd decided to get married as soon as we had found somewhere to live. But when he'd asked me all those questions and studied his lists and his books, he came back shaking his head. He said there was nothing there and we couldn't hope to find a flat this month. At least we've found out it's not going to be easy." Martin sighed. "So – we shall have to be patient. Come on, let's go to the cinema to forget about flats."

As they were going out they met Philippa coming in.

"I say," she called, "has Christina told you about that flat? Her brother Sidney said there was a super one free." Then she suddenly went red and put a hand to her mouth. "Ooh, perhaps I ought not to have told you. Sorry. Forget it."

It was a few days later that Martin next went to Jillian's flat. He had been asking everybody he met if they knew of a flat to rent. He had been watching the newspaper advertisements. He had been thinking, half-seriously, of looking for a job somewhere else. "Since I was here the other day," he said, "I've visited five house agents. I've phoned seven more and I've read the advertisements in fifteen newspapers."

"Perhaps it's a bad time of year," Jillian answered. "I rang my agent again. He said he had been looking for a flat for us, but he hadn't found one the right size. I say, I've just remembered that flat Philippa was talking about so mysteriously the other day. She hasn't said anything more about it."

At that moment Philippa and Christina, looking very pleased with themselves, burst into the room. They hadn't heard Jillian and Martin and stood in the doorway suddenly silent and surprised.

"Hello, you two," Martin called, "come and tell us where to find a flat."

Then Philippa came forward. "Jill," she said, "Sidney found a super flat with two bedrooms. But – I'm sorry – oh, you explain Christina." So Christina told Jillian and Martin that she had got a new job and that she and Philippa didn't want to share a flat with anybody else after Jillian had got married and left. So they were going to move into the flat Sidney had found near Christina's new job.

An unkind thought about her friends filled Jillian's mind. They didn't need this super flat as much as she and Martin did. Then suddenly she

15

had a wonderful idea. "Martin," she said. "Do you see what that means? We can live here, in this flat, if Philippa and Christina are leaving."

Martin jumped up from his chair. "That's marvellous," he said. "Let's get married tomorrow."

They were still talking excitedly a few minutes later when Philippa stopped them. She said that Jillian's house agent had just telephoned to say he had found her a flat. And Christina ran in with the news that a man was at the front door asking for Martin. "He said Martin had asked him to find a flat, and he wanted him to come and look at it," she said.

"Oh dear, that's life," Martin laughed. "One minute you've got nothing, and the next you've got too much."

New words

an armchair, to sigh, to get on, it doesn't matter, enough, during, hopeful, to be able to, patient, to rent, pleased, to burst into, surprised, forward, to move, unkind, a thought, to need, life.

Exercise 6

In the story, Jillian told Martin about her telephone conversation with a house agent. She said:

"I said we were going to get married soon and we wanted a flat. He asked if we wanted a ground floor flat and I told him it didn't matter. He wanted to know if we wanted one bedroom or two, and I said one was enough. Then he said he hadn't got any small flats at the moment. He said he had been looking for a one-bedroom flat for somebody else for five weeks, and he couldn't find one. But I've got his phone number and I promised to ring him up again during the week."

Write out the conversation between Jillian and the agent, using the words they said. Then write out Martin's conversation with his house agent in the High Street.

Exercise 7

When Tom was a young newspaper reporter, he often had to interview people. He always wrote the interview down in his shorthand notebook. Then he wrote it out later for his newspaper editor. Here are his notes of one interview.

15

TOM   Have you had an interesting holiday in America?

SIR JAMES   Yes, I have. I've visited many cities and seen many romantic places.

TOM   How long have you been back?

SIR JAMES   Oh, I've only been home for two hours.

TOM   And what is the most exciting thing you remember?

SIR JAMES   Oh, breaking my leg on the first day. I've been in hospital for three weeks. I've only seen all the cities and romantic places on the television.

Tom's editor told him to start, "When I asked — if —, he told me that —." You try to write Tom's interview story for him. Notice how the newspaper editor likes to use "that", but we don't usually say it in conversation. The editor likes to be more formal.

Exercise 8
Answer all these questions by using "Because".

Why did Jillian and Martin want a flat?
Why did Jillian take the house agent's phone number?
Why did she want to telephone him during the week?
Why did the High Street house agent have a list in his window?
Why did the assistant shake his head to Martin?
Why did Martin and Jillian go to the cinema?
Why did Philippa put a hand to her mouth when she had started talking?
Why had Martin been watching the newspaper advertisements?
Why had Martin been thinking about getting a job somewhere else?
Why did Christina want to move into the new flat?

Now answer all the questions again, but this time use "to — ". (They wanted a flat to live in.)

Finally, answer them again, using "so that — could — ". (They wanted a flat so that they could live in it.)

15

Exercise 9

Ask a friend what he (or she) has done.

Ask him if
{
he has been to*
he has ever seen**
he has ever met***
}

* London, New York, Paris, Rome, Vienna, Stockholm, Warsaw, Moscow, Cairo, Delhi, Tokyo.

** a cricket match, a football match, a tennis match, a swimming gala, a horse race.

*** a newspaper reporter, a jeweller, a pop singer, an insurance agent, a typist.

Then write five sentences like this.

When I asked Maria if she had ever seen a swimming gala, she said she hadn't.

Exercise 10   Conversation practice

A	I've got an awful ache in my	head. knee. back.	What ought I to do?

B	Go to my doctor.	She He	always	tells me knows	what to do. how to make it better.

15

A	Last time I went	she / he	asked me / wanted to know	if I

had ever been to India.
was married.
could go into hospital.

B	Yes	she / he	told a friend of mine he

was never going to walk again.
had to lie on his back for six months.
ought to stop smoking and drinking.

A	Thank you, it doesn't matter. My	head / knee / back	is	fine / better	now.

Unit 16

He said, "I lost it"
He said he had lost it

Martin said, "I saw Margaret. But she didn't see me."
Martin said he had seen Margaret, but she hadn't seen him.

Exercise 1
Look at these people.

1
Martin
got off
a bus.

2
Tom
ran for
the bus.

3
Mary
called
to Tom.

4
Liz stood
and watched
them.

5
Peter
looked at
his watch.

Pretend each one told you what he did. Write four more sentences like: Martin said, "I got off the bus." Then write four more like: Martin said he had got off the bus.

Then ask five questions about the pictures and give five answers. Like this: Did Martin say why he had got off the bus? No, he didn't tell us why he had got off it.

He said, "I shall be late"   **He said, "She will be late"**
He said he would be late   **He said she would be late**

Look again at Martin and Margaret at the beginning of this Unit.

Margaret said to herself, "I shall never speak to him again."
She told herself she would never speak to him again.

Martin said to himself, "She will never look at me."
He told himself she would never look at him.

Exercise 2
Look at the five people in Exercise 1.

Martin thought, "I shall be late."
Tom thought, "I shall catch the bus easily."
Mary thought, "I will bring him back."
Liz thought, "I will never shout after a man."
Peter thought, "I will go in the car for Liz later."

Write one sentence for each picture like this.
Martin: I thought I should be late.

Then ask somebody five questions. Ask:

Who	told	himself herself	he she	would	never shout after a man?
					catch the bus easily?
					be late?
	said				bring Tom back?
					go in the car for Liz later?

Tell them to answer in full sentences.

Exercise 3
Look at these five pictures again, and put these broken sentences together.

1
Tony carrying
a violin

2
Martin getting
a raincoat

3
Tim mending
a ship

16

4
Jillian looking at
a ring

5
Peter and Liz
painting a house

Tony thought he would	never stand under a ladder again.
Martin told himself he would	never be a good violinist.
Tim began to think he would	pay somebody to do the job.
Jillian told herself she would	have to buy a new raincoat.
Peter thought he would	ask Tony to help him another time.
Liz told herself she would	never see a more beautiful ring.

Exercise 4

Look at the five people in Exercise 1 again, and write the exact words they said or thought.

Martin thought he would be late and he wouldn't see Jillian.

Tom told himself the bus wouldn't go without him because the driver would see him.

Mary thought she would make Tom come back. She thought he wouldn't get on the bus if she called.

Liz told herself she would never shout after a man. She would never be like Mary.

Peter thought he would go for Liz after five o'clock, because she wouldn't be ready before that.

Exercise 5

Look back at Martin and Margaret at the beginning of this Unit. Martin said, "She didn't see me."
He said she hadn't seen him.

Now look at the five people in Exercise 1, and write these sentences like:
He said he hadn't seen him.

Martin said, "The bus didn't stop in the right place."
Tom said, "I didn't hear what Mary said."
Mary said, "I didn't want Tom to go."
Liz said, "Tom didn't want to hear Mary."
Peter said, "I didn't think it was time to go for Liz."

The visit

"They'll be here soon," Jillian called from the kitchen. Martin was putting a new bookshelf up in the living-room of her flat. "Yes," he shouted back. "They said they would come between two and half past."

It was a Saturday afternoon. The two girls who had been sharing Jillian's flat had moved into another, and Martin was helping Jillian to clean up, and get the flat ready for their visitors. They had asked Martin's parents to come and see where they were going to live after they had got married.

Suddenly Jillian came into the living-room and said they had forgotten to buy any flowers for the flat. "Didn't you say you would bring some in, darling?" she asked.

"No, I thought you said you would get some. But it doesn't matter," he said. "Mother's got a garden full of daffodils at home. You needn't worry about flowers for her." Then he looked out of the flat window at the small garden, where more daffodils were dancing in the wind.

Jillian started to explain that all the flats shared the garden, but that she had bought the daffodils and put them in, because nobody else had been interested, when somebody rang the door-bell.

"It's them," Jillian said and went to let them in. But it was only Tim and Tony, Martin's little brothers, and they said their parents would be arriving in fifteen or twenty minutes. When she saw them, Jillian had an idea and asked Martin if she might send the boys to get some flowers.

"Of course," he answered, so Jillian gave them some money and told them to be as quick as possible. Tim said they would try to get back with the flowers before their parents arrived.

"You needn't worry," Tony said, "we shall be here first."

A quarter of an hour later the twins were back. "We told you we should get here first," Tim said, giving a bunch of daffodils to Jillian. As she started putting them in a vase, the boys asked if they might go and play in the park that was round the corner. Martin said they might. "But don't be late home, then," he called after them, wondering why they were in such a big hurry.

"That's funny," Jillian suddenly burst out. "Have you ever bought a bunch of seventeen daffodils, Martin?" He told her he usually bought a dozen or two dozen but never seventeen. And as he was speaking, a sudden thought hit him. And he knew the boys hadn't bought the flowers. He rushed across the room to the vase to have a careful look at the daffodils. They were just like those in the garden at home. And as he opened his mouth to speak, the door-bell rang.

Jillian walked slowly to the door to answer it, while Martin told her as quickly as possible that he thought the boys had got the daffodils from their father's garden, that his father would be very angry and that he mustn't see the flowers. And as Jillian opened the front door to let Martin's parents in, Martin rushed with the vase of daffodils into the kitchen and pushed it into a cupboard.

16

For the next half hour Martin watched Jillian with admiration as she asked his parents to let her take their coats, told them to make themselves comfortable and asked if they would have a cup of tea. When Jillian showed them round the flat, they both said it was a comfortable place to start married life in. Then, just before Martin's parents left, Jillian came out of the kitchen with the bunch of daffodils the boys had brought. She had put them in some pretty paper, and now gave them to Martin's mother, telling her she knew how much she liked flowers. The visit was a great success.

When his parents had left, Martin turned to Jillian and asked what she thought his father would say when he got home and found the daffodils were from his own garden. She smiled. "If the twins took them from your garden, they ought to go back to your house," she said. "But come here." And she took him to the window and pointed to her small garden, where somebody had cut all the daffodils. "There were seventeen," she said, sadly.

The next morning Martin's father rang Jillian to say that he had noticed the empty garden, and wanted to give Jillian some flowers to look at. He asked if he might come and put them in her garden for her, and the twins said they would come and help. Jillian smiled sweetly into the telephone and said she understood.

New words

a visit, to put up, a visitor, darling, a daffodil, interested, to let in, possible, a bunch, a vase, to wonder, such, a dozen, to rush, admiration, a success.

Exercise 6

The first time Jillian stayed in a hotel she asked all these questions.

May I have breakfast at half past seven?
May I have two eggs for breakfast?
May I have a shower?
May I have a television in my room?
May I use the phone?
May I bring my friends into the hotel?
May I tell my friends to write to me here?

May I use the lift?
May I stay until the end of the month?
May I have my bill?

Make ten new sentences from these, beginning: Jillian asked if she might — . *or* The manager told her she might (not) — .

Exercise 7

Give the conversation when Jillian asked Martin's mother to let her take her coat, told her to make herself comfortable and asked if she would have a cup of tea. Also when Jillian showed her round the flat.

Now make another conversation between yourself and a friend who is paying a visit to your home for the first time.

Exercise 8

Read the story again and then answer these questions.

Why had they asked Martin's parents to pay a visit to Jillian's flat?
Why hadn't they bought any flowers to put in the flat?
Why did Martin say it didn't matter that there were no flowers?
Why did Jillian put daffodils in the garden of the flats?
How did the twins know when their parents would be arriving?
How did Tony know they would get back with the flowers before their parents?
How did Jillian know the boys hadn't bought the daffodils from a shop?
Why did Martin put the daffodils in a cupboard?
Why did Jillian give them to Martin's mother?
Why did the twins say they would help their father in Jillian's garden?

Exercise 9

Martin can't live without sleep. He must sleep. He has to sleep. But there's a correct time to sleep. He mustn't sleep at the office. He ought not to sleep there. When he's sleeping in bed he always wears green pyjamas. He needn't wear green pyjamas, but he does.

Now say five sentences about things you must do, five sentences about things you mustn't do, and five sentences about things you needn't do.

16

Exercise 10   Conversation practice

A	I was wondering if X had spoken to you yesterday. Did X speak to you yesterday?

B	Yes, he said he had been looking forward to seeing me. Yes. He said, "I've been looking forward to seeing you."

Why do you ask?

A	The other day	he told me he would never speak to you again. he said, "I'll never speak to B again."

Unit 17

I may get lost

Perhaps it will rain.
It's possible it will
  rain.
It may rain.
Or it may not.

Perhaps I shall climb it.
It's possible I shall
  climb it.
I may climb it.
Or I may not.

Perhaps I shall win.
It's possible I shall
  win.
I may win.
Or I may not.

Exercise 1
Look at these five pictures again.

1
Martin
got off
a bus.

2
Tom
ran for
the bus.

3
Mary
called
to Tom.

4
Liz stood
and watched
them.

5
Peter
looked at
his watch.

17

Who is thinking these sentences?

I may catch the bus.
The bus driver may not wait for him.
He may like her calling after him.
I may be early for Jillian.
I may not catch the bus.
The bus may go without him.
Liz may have shut the shop when I arrive.
He may not be listening to her.
I may be late for Jillian.
She may not have shut the shop when I arrive.

Exercise 2

At the beginning of this Unit, Jillian thought perhaps it would rain. She told herself it might rain or it might not. Tom thought he might climb the tree or he might not. Peter said he might win or he might not.

Now write ten sentences, using "might", from the sentences in Exercise 1. Like this: Tom thought he might catch the bus.

Exercise 3

Finish these sentences, using either "may" or "might".

When I take an examination I always tell my friends, "I — pass and I — not."
When I take an examination I always tell my friends I — pass and I — not.
When I go to the dentist's I always think he — not take any teeth out.
When I go to the dentist's I always say, "He — not take any teeth out."
When I started reading my last book I thought, "I — not finish this."
When I lose things I always tell myself I — find them again.
When I say goodbye to people I think I — never see them again.
When people ask me to meet them, I always say, "I — be late."

17

I might get lost

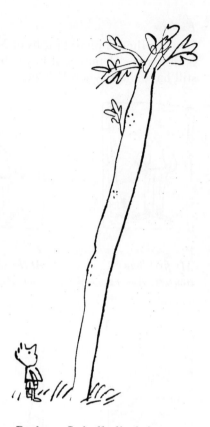

Perhaps it will rain,
but I don't think it will.
It might rain.

Perhaps I shall climb it,
but I don't think so.
I might climb it.

Perhaps I shall win, but I don't think so. I might win.

17

Exercise 4

Look at the six photographs of Martin again. In the first photograph he is thinking, "I may still have these trousers when I'm 13. And I might still have them when I'm 23."

1
*My first long
trousers. Age 12.*

2
*At the swimming
pool. Age 8.*

3
*After my first driving
lesson. Age 17.*

4
*An early walk
with Jill. Age 20.*

5
*My first car.
Age 21.*

6
*In the mountains.
Age 21.*

Now finish the following sentences using either "may" or "might".

In the second photograph he is thinking, "I — be a very good swimmer next year and I — be a good one next week."

In the third photograph he is thinking, "My driving teacher — not give me any more lessons but he — forget this accident before next week."

In the fourth photograph he is thinking, "I — be doing this again tomorrow and I — still be doing it in twenty years' time."

In the fifth photograph he is thinking, "I — get a new car every year, and I — get a new girl friend every year too."

In the sixth photograph he is thinking, "I — climb three or four more mountains before tea, or I — just sit here."

I wrote to John, who wrote back

Who are these five people?

1

2

3

4

5

The first is Martin, who is getting off a bus.

The second is Tom, who is running after the bus, which is just starting to move.

The third is Mary, who is calling after Tom.

The fourth is Liz, who is watching Mary.

The fifth is Peter, who is looking at his watch, which has stopped.

17

Exercise 5

Who can you think of in this book? Think of ten people and write three sentences for each, like this.

There is Christina. She lived with Jillian. There's Christina, who lived with Jillian.

Getting ready for the wedding

Once they had decided to get married, Jillian and Martin began to work on their wedding plans. They decided to go to Paris for their honeymoon. So they visited the local travel agent, who said, "Yes, I think there may be two seats free on the afternoon plane on April 3rd. And there's a very good hotel I know that may have a room. Leave it with me, please. I'll let you know."

Then they went round to the local church to talk about the wedding. They met the vicar, who looked in his diary. "April 3rd?" he said. "It's possible. I may be free then. But there are so many young people who want to get married. Ah yes, there's one wedding at one o'clock. Will half-past one be a good time?" And Jillian and Martin said it would.

Jillian's father, who had to pay for the reception, took her to see the manager of a local hotel. They asked him if they could have the wedding reception there. He said he thought nobody had booked his large room for the date they wanted. "It may be free," he said, looking in a notebook. "Ah, yes. I thought so. It is."

They telephoned the local taxi service and asked if they might use their cars for the wedding. They rang the local florist's and asked if they could have two dozen red roses. "It's rather early in the year," the assistant said, "but we may get some for you. We'll do what we can."

Then Martin asked Tom if he would be the best man at the wedding. "You know," he explained, "you are the one who makes sure everything goes right. You look after the ring, and stand with me in church, and pay the taxi men." Tom said he would be very happy to be Martin's best man, but he couldn't do it on April 3rd.

"Then, we'll have to change the date, shan't we, Jill darling?" Martin said. "Let's bring the wedding forward one week."

17

So he and Jillian started telephoning.

"You want your flowers a week earlier?" the florist said. "It may be rather difficult. But we'll try. Of course, the roses may cost a little more. But we'll see what we can do."

"You want your booking a week earlier?" the taxi man said. "The cars may be free then. I shall have to look in the book. I'll let you know later."

"Bring your wedding date forward?" the hotel manager asked. "I'm not sure. I may have another reception on the date you want. But I'll do my best for you."

"You want to get married on March 27th?" the vicar said. "Oh, dear. Other people may have asked for that day. I'll have to look in my diary, then I'll phone you back. It may be possible, or it may not."

"Your honeymoon's going to be earlier?" the travel agent said. "But all the seats may have gone on the earlier plane. And somebody else may have booked your room in the hotel for that week. But I'll ring up and find out at once."

The next day everybody telephoned back to Martin. They all said they could change the date of the wedding, except the travel agent, who couldn't book new plane seats or a new hotel room.

"So now," said Jillian, "we've got a wedding in March, but we can't start our honeymoon until April 3rd. If your friend, Tom, can't come on the right date, we shall have to get married without him. Come on, Martin, we must ask all those people to change the date back again to April 3rd." They rushed to the telephone.

"Change back to April 3rd?" the vicar said. "That might still be possible, but I don't think so. No, somebody else has asked me to marry them. I'm sorry."

"Put the date back again?" the hotel manager asked. "The large reception room might still be free, but I don't think so. No. Somebody else has booked it for the time you wanted it."

"A week later, now?" the taxi man said. "My cars might all be free, but I have an idea they're not. No. Somebody else has asked for them for the day you want them."

"You want your roses in April now?" the florist asked. "We might have some more coming, but I think we've promised the ones you cancelled to somebody else. Yes, that's right. I'm sorry. And we can't get any more."

When everything went wrong, Jillian began to cry; and at the same time, Tom rang the door-bell. As Martin let him in, Jillian ran away and shut

17

herself in the bathroom. Tom listened with a long face as Martin told him
how all their plans had gone wrong, and explained that they might have
to cancel the wedding until later. Then Tom sadly told Martin why he
had come. He had been going to get married, too, on April 3rd. He was
keeping it a secret, and that was why he hadn't been able to be Martin's
best man that day. But now his girlfriend had changed her mind and
there wasn't going to be a wedding. So he was free on April 3rd.

"But," said Martin patiently, "the vicar, the reception room and the
taxis aren't free. And there are no red roses left for the day we want."

"There will be now," Tom said. "I'm just going to cancel all mine.
You two may have my wedding time – one o'clock – with the same vicar.
You may have my booking for the same reception room and the same
taxis. And you may have my red roses from the florist. But," he said,
sighing, "I may not feel like being your best man, Martin. May I have
a week or two to think about it?"

New words

a wedding, a plan, a honeymoon, local, a church, a vicar, a reception,
large, a service, a florist, except, a secret, to be able, patiently.

Exercise 6

Read these sentences from the story.

The florist said, "It may be rather difficult. But we'll try. Of course, the
roses may cost a little more. But we'll see what we can do."
The taxi man said, "The cars may be free then. I shall have to look in the
book. I'll let you know later."
The hotel manager said, "I'm not sure. I may have another reception on
the date you want. But I'll do my best for you."
The vicar said, "Other people may have asked for that day. I'll have to
look in my diary, then I'll phone you back. It may be possible or it
may not."
The travel agent said, "All the seats may have gone on the earlier plane.
And somebody else may have booked your room in the hotel for that
week. But I'll ring up and find out at once."

Write out what the five people said, but without using their exact words.
Like this: The florist said it might be rather difficult. But they would try.

17

Exercise 7

When Jillian and Martin telephoned all the people the second time, who told them somebody else had asked for the large reception room? Who had booked it?

Who said somebody else had booked the cars? Who had asked for them?

Who said he had promised the roses to somebody else? Who had asked for them?

Who told them somebody else had asked him to marry them? Do we know who it was?

Do you think Martin was right for wanting to change the date?
Do you think Jillian was right for letting Martin change the date?
Do you think Tom was silly for having a girl who changed her mind?

Exercise 8

Practise asking people: Where will you be at this time tomorrow?

Answer: I shall be — *. *or* I may be — **. *or* I might be — ***. *or* I shan't be — *.
* (certainly)   ** (perhaps)   *** (just possibly)

Now ask:

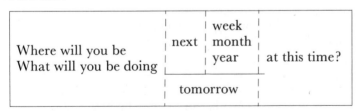

Where will you be What will you be doing	next	week month year	at this time?
		tomorrow	

17

Exercise 9

Read these sentences Jillian has written, then make up sentences like them about your own dentist, etc.

My dentist, who lives not far away, doesn't like taking teeth out.
Our local florist's, which is usually full of flowers, hasn't had any roses lately.
My local church, which is only round the corner, has some beautiful windows.
Our family doctor, who usually rushes round when we need him, couldn't visit us the last time we telephoned.
The launderette we use, which is full except at lunch-time, has got the largest machines in the town.
My nearest travel agent, who usually sells me plane tickets, shuts on Wednesday afternoons.
Our local taxi service, which is more expensive to use than the train, is slower.
My hairdresser, who always listens patiently to what I say, does whatever she likes with my hair.
Our cleaner, who looked after the flat when Chris and Philippa lived with me, is called Mrs Brass.
My wedding, which takes place on April 3rd, is going to cost a lot of money.

Exercise 10   Conversation practice

A	Do you know Can you tell me	if X	is coming will be here	tonight? today?

B	I'm not sure;	he said he would come, so he ought to be here soon. he was ill last week, but he may be better now. he was ill earlier today, but he might be better now.

A	He said	he would lend me his I might borrow his he would let me have his	notebook exercise book homework	to take home. to follow. to copy from.

17

B	Oh, don't	follow copy	him. his work.

He	followed copied borrowed	my	notebook, exercise book, homework,	and that which	was all wrong.

Unit 18

Having spoken, he sat down

When Martin had heard the weather forecast, he took his raincoat.
Martin, having heard the weather forecast, took his raincoat.
Having heard the weather forecast, Martin took his raincoat.

Exercise 1
Look at these five people again, and read these sentences.

1
Martin got off
a bus.

2
Tom ran for
the bus.

3
Mary called
to Tom.

4
Liz stood and
watched them.

5
Peter looked at
his watch.

Martin pushed the bell and got off the bus.
Tom saw the bus and ran to catch it.
Mary saw Tom and called after him.
Liz came to the shop door and watched them.
Peter thought about Liz and looked at his watch.

Now write those sentences again in two ways, first beginning "When Martin had" and then beginning with "Having".

Exercise 2
Now finish these sentences.

Having read (the title of a book), I think — .
Having seen (the title of a film), I think — .
Having met (the name of a person), I feel sure — .
Having been to (the name of a place), I want — .
Having eaten in (the name of a restaurant), I know — .
Having read my first English book, I thought — .
Having seen my first film, I thought — .
Having met my first teacher, I felt sure — .
Having been to my first party, I wanted — .
Having eaten in my first restaurant, I knew — .

I may have lost it

Martin can't find his ball pen.
Perhaps he has lost it.
He may have lost it.

Exercise 3

How many more sentences can you make about the picture? Write five.

He			put it in his pocket.
Susan	may		left it at the office.
Sandy	might	have	borrowed it.
His mother			taken it into the garden.
			thrown it away.

Now write five things you might say when you can't find something.
Start with "I may have".

18

Exercise 4

Look again at the ten sentences you have written in the last exercise. Write the same ideas again, but this time start, "I thought Martin (etc.) might have — ."

The great day

It was the day of Jillian and Martin's wedding. Having arrived early at the church, Martin sat down at the front listening to the music, and Tom, who was his best man, sat silently beside him. Martin looked at his watch – it was three minutes to one. Jillian would be arriving, he told himself, very soon. And then the thought came back into his mind that he had forgotten something. What could it be? He might have forgotten to get the money to give Tom for the taxis. But no, he could feel it in the inside pocket of the suit he had hired for the wedding. He wondered if he had got his passport ready at home. He might have forgotten to put it with everything else he needed for the honeymoon. But no, he knew he had done that. It wasn't his passport that he had forgotten.

At that moment the Wedding March rang through the church and Jillian and her father, who had arrived by taxi at the church door, began to walk slowly towards Martin. Having arrived at his side, she gave him a quick look and a secret smile, then turned to listen to the vicar, who was starting to speak.

"She ought to wear white more often," Martin thought. "I wonder what she's thinking now. She might be wondering if she's doing the right thing. Oh, what is it that I've forgotten?" He began to wonder if he had given the ring to Tom, who was standing just behind him. He might have left the ring in his other suit at home. But, no, Tom had shown him the ring in the taxi. Then suddenly he realized that the vicar was speaking to him.

"Will you, Martin, have this woman to be your wedded wife?"

"I will," he answered faintly, and all thoughts disappeared from his mind.

18

Ten minutes later he stood with Jillian, smiling patiently, outside the church door, while the photographer pushed their parents into a group beside them. "I may not have packed my camera," he thought, "or they might not sell my particular films in Paris."

"Stop worrying," Jillian told him in the taxi, which was taking them to the wedding reception.

"But I feel sure I've forgotten something," he said. "I think I might have lost the plane tickets. Or I might not have got enough money for the honeymoon. Or something."

Soon they were at the local hotel and all their friends and relations, having followed them from the church in cars and taxis, started to shake hands and say "Congratulations" and everybody wanted to kiss the bride. The wedding reception began, but all the time Martin was still wondering if he had forgotten anything. "I may not have packed those new orange pyjamas I bought. I may not have written down the address of the hotel we're staying at."

Having left their friends still drinking wine and eating wedding cake at the reception, Jillian and Martin went to change their clothes, and get ready for going away. Still Martin couldn't think of anything he had forgotten. Their passports and tickets were with his own suit, where he had put them. His camera and new orange pyjamas were in his case, where he had packed them. The address of their Paris hotel was in his wallet, which he had put in the inside pocket of his own suit.

Soon they were at the airport. They were sitting close together, waiting for their plane, when Martin suddenly remembered. "I know what I haven't done, darling," he shouted and rushed to the nearest telephone box. He was back at Jillian's side a moment later, smiling. "I had forgotten to ask Tom to take that wedding suit back to the shop I hired it from," he said.

"Well," Jillian answered. "I'm glad you've remembered. Now you might start thinking about us and stop wondering what you've forgotten."

Half an hour later, their plane was high in the air. Suddenly Martin let go of Jillian's hand, having remembered that he had not told Tom about the taxi money he had left in the pocket of his wedding suit. Tom wouldn't think to look in the pockets before he took the suit back. Martin sighed.

"What's the matter, darling?" Jillian asked.

"Nothing, darling," he answered. "I'm just looking forward to married life with you."

New words
silently, beside, a suit, to hire, a passport, a smile, to realize, wedded, to disappear, a relation, a bride, orange, close, to let go.

Exercise 5
Here is the list of what happened to Jillian and Martin on their wedding day.

arrived at church; got married; stood patiently at the church door for the photographer; went to the hotel for the reception; drank wine and ate wedding cake with their friends and relations; changed their clothes; drove to the airport; flew to Paris.

Say six more sentences like this: When they had arrived at church, they got married.
Then write about the same things in seven sentences, all starting "Having".

18

Exercise 6

Think about what you have done today, and write a list. Then make sentences with two things from your list in each, using either "When I had" or "Having".

Exercise 7

Read the story again, then answer these questions.

What does a best man do at a wedding?
Who travels to church with the bride?
Who looks after the wedding ring?
What happens at a wedding reception?
What time was Jillian's wedding?
What colour was her wedding dress?
Who else was at the wedding?
Why do you think they needed to change their clothes?
Why do you think Martin wanted Tom to take the suit back as soon as possible?
What do you think happened to the taxi money in the suit pocket?

Exercise 8

Finish these sentences.

Tom, who — , sat beside Martin.
The vicar, who — , stood in front of them.
Jillian, who — , gave him a secret smile.
She came and stood beside Martin, who — .
They smiled patiently at the photographer, who — .
Martin's wedding suit, which — , had the taxi money in an inside pocket.
Martin had packed his orange pyjamas, which — .
His passport, which — , was with his own suit.
The hotel address was in his wallet, which — .
Martin realized the money was still in the suit, which — .

18

Exercise 9

Write two short sentences about each of the following: your best friend, your father, your job, your bedroom, your favourite sport.

Then join your two short sentences into one longer one, using "who" or "which". Like this:

My best friend is sitting beside me now. He often helps me with my work.
My best friend, who often helps me with my work, is sitting beside me now.

Exercise 10   Conversation practice

A	I can't find my watch. My watch has disappeared.	I was wondering if you had seen it. I don't know what I've done with it.

B	Well, you've been to the cinema.	You might Perhaps you	have lost it there.

A	Yes,	I might. that's true.	Or, I may have left it at the swimming pool.

B	Or	perhaps somebody has somebody might have	borrowed it.

A	Of course, I've just	realized. remembered.

My	sister brother	may have taken it.	I said	she he	might. could.

Practise the conversation again, but instead of a watch, talk about something of your own. And instead of the cinema and swimming pool, talk about places you've visited today.

Unit 19

The man watching us

Here's another photograph of Jillian's wedding.
The girl getting into the car is Jillian.
The man helping her is Martin.
The two little boys putting a notice on the back of the car are Martin's
   little brothers.
The girl walking away is Margaret.

Exercise 1
Look at the two pictures again on page 183. Practise in twos.

ONE SAYS   There's a man waiting at the library counter.

THE OTHER SAYS   Is the man waiting at the library counter in picture 1
or picture 2?

THE FIRST ONE SAYS   The man waiting at the library counter is in picture 2.

Now talk in the same way about these people:

the girl standing behind the library counter
the man talking on the telephone.
the woman reading a book

the man carrying a bunch of flowers
the man carrying a stick
the child carrying a book
the child buying stamps
the woman selling stamps
the man selling stamps
the woman putting something away in her bag

Exercise 2
The last time Jillian went to Martin's house, Tony asked her if she would draw for him. When she asked what he wanted her to draw, the first thing he said was, "Draw a horse riding a bicycle."

Can you think of ten more silly ideas that Tony might have had? Each one must be something (like a horse) doing something (like riding a bicycle).

I heard you coming

In the picture at the beginning of this Unit,

The twins were putting a notice on the car.
Martin didn't see them putting the notice on the car.
Jillian was getting into the car.
The driver didn't see her getting into the car.
But he heard her getting into the car.
Martin was helping her.
She didn't see him helping her. But she felt him holding her.
Margaret was walking away. But Martin didn't notice her going.

19

Exercise 3

How many questions can you ask? Practise in twos.

Have you ever	seen heard watched listened to	— *	playing? talking? singing? dancing?

* the names of famous musicians, sportsmen, actors, singers, dancers, politicians.

If the answer is yes, say:

Yes,	he she	was	playing talking singing dancing	on the	television radio
				in the	town hall local theatre
					(etc.)

when I	saw heard watched listened to	him. her.

19

I heard you come

A man was climbing this mountain and two people were watching him: the man looking through binoculars at the foot of the mountain and the cameraman filming in the helicopter. But halfway up the mountain there were clouds.

When the climber was climbing below the clouds, the man with the binoculars saw him.
The man with the binoculars saw him climbing below the clouds.

When the climber climbed to the hut, the man with the binoculars saw him.
The man with the binoculars saw him climb to the hut.

When he was climbing above the clouds, the cameraman saw him.
The cameraman saw him climbing above the clouds.

When he climbed to the top of the mountain, the cameraman saw him.
The cameraman saw him climb to the top of the mountain.

19

Exercise 4
Write answers to these questions, using full sentences.

Who could see the climber start from the foot of the mountain?
(The cameraman? The helicopter pilot? The man with the binoculars?)

Who could see the climber arrive at the hut?
(The man filming in the helicopter? The man watching through binoculars?)

Who could watch the climber getting near the top?
(The man using the film camera? The pilot flying the helicopter? The man standing at the bottom?)

Who could see the climber get to the top?
(The man flying in the helicopter? The man standing on the ground?)

Who could hear the helicopter flying above the clouds?
(The man with the binoculars? The climber?)

Who could see the helicopter flying above the clouds?
(The man watching through binoculars? The man climbing near the mountain top?)

Exercise 5
Look back to the wedding picture at the beginning of this Unit.
When Margaret was there, Jillian was getting into the taxi, Martin was helping her, the taxi driver was sitting in the driver's seat, the twins were making a noise behind the car, and Tom was standing watching.

Write four more sentences about Margaret, like: Margaret saw Jillian getting into the taxi.

But after Margaret left, Martin and Jillian got into the taxi, the boys put the notice on the back, the driver started the car, and the car moved away.

Write four more sentences about Tom, like: Tom saw Margaret leave.
Use "see", "hear", "notice", "watch".

Trouble with a letter

It happened on the ninth day of Jillian's honeymoon in Paris. She came down the hotel stairs, singing to herself, to wait for Martin, who had gone out shopping. Having looked round the entrance hall and smiled at the French girl sitting behind the reception desk filing her nails, she sat down with a newspaper for a moment, pretending to read. But her eye kept coming back to the receptionist, the hair falling over her face, the hotel book lying open on the desk beside her and the letters waiting on the wall behind her, waiting for people to come for them.

Then suddenly she saw something that sent the blood rushing to her cheeks. One of the letters behind the receptionist was for her. But instead of her married name, Mrs M. Fry, the name on the envelope was Miss J. Grey. She sat for minutes, looking over the receptionist's shoulder at the blue envelope of the air letter, carrying an English stamp in the top right-hand corner. Who could have written to her, she wondered, desperately? Who could have known where they were staying? And who could have been so careless as to use her old name? But the important thing to do was to get the letter now, without the receptionist knowing.

"I don't want to go telling everybody I've just got married," she told herself. "Somehow I must make that girl leave the desk for a minute."

The receptionist heard Jillian coming to the desk, but she didn't look up. "Yes, Mrs Fry?" she asked, as she sat still filing her nails.

"I would like to speak to the manager," Jillian said rather desperately. "Will you go and see if he's in his office, please?"

"I'm sorry," the girl said with a sigh. "He's just gone out. I saw him go. Didn't you hear him walk across the hall a minute ago? Would you like me to tell you when he comes back?"

"Oh don't worry, thank you," Jillian answered. And with a new plan coming into her mind, she walked quickly to the back of the entrance hall. There, under the stairs, behind a door with a little window, she had noticed a telephone. Looking back over her shoulder, she saw the receptionist working on her nails again. In a moment Jillian was behind the door and lifting the phone. She saw the receptionist pick up hers.

"This is Mrs Fry," Jillian said. "Please come up to my room for a moment," and she put the phone down. She watched the French girl shake her head, then saw her walk uncertainly across the hall, and heard her climb the stairs above her.

In a minute Jillian was back in the hall. She rushed round the reception desk and took the letter in both hands. But as she stood holding it thankfully, she heard somebody coming through the hotel entrance. There was no time to move, so having dropped to the floor on her hands and knees, she hid under the desk. She heard the person come into the entrance hall and sit down. She heard him looking through a newspaper and then singing quietly to himself. It was Martin!

But before she could stand up or let him know she was there, she heard the receptionist coming downstairs again. Jillian pulled herself as far as possible under the desk, as she saw the French girl's legs appear beside her.

Nobody spoke. Then Jillian heard Martin put his newspaper down, get up from his chair and go upstairs. Then the receptionist's smiling face appeared. "You can come out now, Mrs Fry," she said. "Your husband has gone upstairs. You were hiding from him, I know. Let me help you."

Jillian tried to laugh. "Thank you," she said, hiding the envelope behind her. Then she went running up the stairs to join Martin and show him the letter.

19

The receptionist stood shaking her head. "Oh these English!" she said.

A young English student, who was working in the hotel for a few months, came in at that moment. "Hello Joyce," the receptionist said. "That Mrs Fry was hiding from her husband under my desk. And the manager says they are on their honeymoon. Do all English people play games like that?" Then realizing that the English girl was thinking about something else, she said, "Ah yes, you've come for your usual letter from your boy friend in England. It's here somewhere – Miss J. Grey. That's funny, I'm sure it was here waiting for you. What can have happened to it?"

New words

to sing, an entrance, a reception desk, to file, a nail, to keep doing something, a receptionist, a cheek, desperately, important, somehow, I would like . . . , a sigh, uncertainly, thankfully, to hide, to appear, a student.

Exercise 6

Look at the picture in the story. Ask a friend:

Who can you see { sitting? / standing? / reading? }

What can you see { standing / lying } on the reception desk?

Who can you see { filing her nails? / pretending to read a newspaper? }

How many people can you see working hard in the picture?

Is there anybody { walking past? / coming into the hotel? }

Exercise 7

Having read the story again, answer these questions.

Why do you think Jillian came downstairs singing?
Why didn't she want to tell the receptionist the letter was hers?
Why did she ask to speak to the manager?
Why did she ask the receptionist to go to her room?
Why did the receptionist walk uncertainly across the hall?

Why couldn't Jillian let Martin know where she was?
Why do you think Martin was waiting in the entrance hall?
What did the receptionist think Jillian was doing under the desk?
Why did Jillian try to laugh?
Why couldn't the receptionist find the student's air letter?

Exercise 8

Pretend a rich relation wants to spend money on you. Give answers to these questions he asks you.

Where would you like to eat this evening?
What would you like to eat?
What would you like to drink?
Is there anybody you'd like to meet?
What would you like for your next birthday?
Where would you like to spend your summer holidays?
Which countries would you like to visit?
Is there a job you would like to have instead of your own?

Exercise 9

Ask somebody these questions:

If you hear somebody trying to get into your house when you are in bed, do you (a) hide? (b) pick up something heavy? (c) run to the telephone?
If you notice somebody drive away in a car that is somebody else's, do you (a) tell the police? (b) drive after him? (c) take no notice?
If you feel somebody take something out of your pocket, do you (a) shout for help? (b) take hold of their arm? (c) see how big they are first?
If you see somebody wearing exactly the same clothes as yours, do you (a) stay well away from them? (b) pretend to be twins? (c) ask how much they paid?
If you find somebody sitting in your place, do you (a) take no notice and sit somewhere else? (b) sit on their knee? (c) ask them politely to move?

19

Exercise 10   Conversation practice

PATIENT | Doctor, I keep on hearing | voices calling. / a voice shouting.

Can you | give me something / tell me how | to stop it?

DOCTOR | Well, | I'd like to hear / you must tell me | more about it. When

do the voices start? / do you hear the voices?

PATIENT | It's funny. I only hear | the voices / somebody | calling / shouting | when I'm

playing / practising | the | violin. / piano.

DOCTOR | That's | interesting. / funny. | Do you know | Mr Smith? / Mrs Jones? / Miss Robinson?

PATIENT | Oh, yes | he / she | lives in the flat | next door to / above | mine. / me.

DOCTOR | He / She | asked me for something to | make her sleep. / help him to sleep.

PATIENT | But why?

19

| DOCTOR | Somebody keeps on playing the | violin / piano | and won't stop |

| playing / practising | even when | he / she | calls. / shouts. |

| PATIENT | Ah, | thank you doctor. / I understand. |

| The | voices / shouting | I can hear | is / are | from | his / her / the next | flat. |

| DOCTOR | Are you going to | keep on / stop | practising? |

| PATIENT | Oh, | yes. / no. | Now I can | play / practise | without worrying where the |

| shouting / voice | is coming from. |

Unit 20

Stop shouting

Here's a group of people in a train. Some of them have started talking. Two have started reading and one has started eating.

Exercise 1

Look at the group of people again. Write full sentences in answer to these questions.

Who started eating before the train left? Who began reading? Who began
    smoking? Who began talking?
When the train started, who stopped talking? Who finished eating? Who
    stopped looking out of the window?
Who was worried about having a hole in her stocking? Who was thinking
    about saying goodbye? Who was still talking about buying clothes?

Start your answers with one of the following: "The young lady holding a
shopping basket", "The young lady wearing a hat", "The man sitting
with the young ladies", "The man standing at the door", "The man
travelling with the large case", "The old lady sitting on the right".

194

20

Exercise 2

After the train had started, which person in the picture do you think said, or thought:

I felt like having something to eat.
I wish he would stop smoking.
I didn't like saying goodbye to her.
I'm looking forward to finishing this book.
I like using that supermarket.
I don't like travelling with people who smoke.
I shall keep on smoking until they say something.
I'll practise using my new typewriter as soon as I get home.
I don't like this hat she keeps on wearing.
I'm not looking forward to carrying that case again.

Skiing is fun

A few weeks after her wedding, Jillian met Tom, who started talking about skiing.

"Oh yes," he said, "I love skiing. There's nothing I like better than rushing over the snow down a good ski slope. I began learning to ski when I was twelve and I was an instructor when I was twenty." Jillian's eyes opened wide.

"I didn't know that," she answered. "Is it easy?"

"Well," Tom said, "you have to practise holding your sticks and turning. You must think about keeping your feet together and a few other things. Have you seen Martin ski? He's quite good at skiing."

The thought came to Jillian that perhaps she ought to learn. It would be fun, she thought, to start having lessons secretly and give Martin a surprise. Then they could go skiing together.

"I say, Tom," she said excitedly, "would you mind teaching me? Would you mind giving me a few skiing lessons?"

But just at that moment Tom remembered something he had to do, and left in a hurry.

20

For the next few days, Jillian kept on thinking about having lessons, and when she saw a notice advertising an artificial ski slope in one of the London parks, she went round and put her name down for a beginners' class, starting the following Monday evening. "Martin mustn't find out where I'm going," she told herself. "I'll just say I've started another evening class and he needn't know what I'm learning."

So she told Martin, at tea-time on Monday, that she had joined a new evening class and would be home at nine o'clock.

"Oh, good," he said, thinking she was talking about studying Spanish, or practising shorthand. "I mustn't ask her too much about it. Just because we're married, she needn't tell me everything she's doing. And, in any case, I can go and have a drink with Tom."

But that evening, Tom was obviously worrying about something. At last he said, "Martin, there's something you ought to know and I can't put off telling you any longer. You see, I happened to be talking to Jillian a few days ago and I told her you were very good at skiing. I'm sorry – I hope you don't mind."

Martin laughed and said, "Oh dear, I've never worn a pair of skis in my life. But it doesn't matter. Let's have another drink."

But later, driving home in the car, he kept on thinking about skiing. "What a silly thing to say!" he thought. "And what will Jill think?" Then he realized that she needn't know he couldn't ski. He remembered hearing somebody talking about an artificial ski slope in London. "That's it," he told himself. "I'll go and have lessons."

So the next day, Martin went round to the ski centre and put his name down for a beginners' class, starting the following Wednesday evening.

"Must I buy a pair of skis and boots?" he asked.

"No," the man said, "you needn't. You may hire them here from us."

For several weeks after that, Jillian went skiing on Mondays and Martin went on Wednesdays. They both kept on practising hard and looked forward to going each week. Then one week Jillian said to Martin, "Oh darling, Wednesday's your evening out, isn't it? So you don't mind if I'm not at home next Wednesday, do you? You see, my instructor can't take our class this Monday, so he's put us with another class that's on Wednesday."

There were a lot of people practising on the artificial ski slope that Wednesday evening. And Jillian arrived at the top, ready to go down, when she turned her head and found Martin at her side.

"What are you doing here?" she began, but the instructor shouted,

20

"Come on, Mrs Fry, quickly please." She started moving down the slope, with Martin following. "I thought you were good at skiing," she called over her shoulder. He laughed, trying to catch up with her.

"Be careful, you two," the instructor called. "There's that silly young man playing about at the bottom of the slope. He's a beginner. Look where you're going."

But it was too late. A moment later Jillian, Martin and the other man were lying in a heap at the bottom of the ski slope, skis, ski sticks, arms and legs everywhere. Then Martin started laughing.

"You needn't laugh," Jillian said, "let's help this other chap, he's only a beginner." They went to where he was lying, still, on his face.

"I say," Jillian said, "we're terribly sorry. Let's give you a hand." The man turned over slowly and looked at them guiltily. It was Tom.

Martin kept on laughing and laughing and all at once the three of them started desperately trying to explain.

New words

to ski, fun, snow, a ski, a slope, an instructor, secretly, would you mind . . . , artificial, a beginner, in any case, obviously, to mind, a centre, several, to catch up with, a heap, a chap, still, all at once.

20

Exercise 3

Tom said, "I began learning to ski when I was twelve." How many true
sentences can you make like that one?

I	began started stopped finished	learning * playing practising	**	when I was — .

* English, typing, shorthand, music, to drive, to read, to ski, to swim.
** football, tennis, the piano, the violin, the guitar.

Exercise 4

Having read the story again, answer these questions.

How do you know Tom was not telling Jillian the truth about skiing?
Why did Jillian keep her skiing lessons a secret?
Why did Martin keep his a secret from Jillian?
Where did Martin think Jillian was going on Mondays?
Where did Jillian think Martin was going on Wednesdays?
Why do you think the instructor told Jillian to be quick?
Why was Jillian surprised to see Martin at the ski centre?
How do you know that it was Martin who first realized what had happened?
Why did Tom look guilty?
Who do you think needed to do the most explaining? And why?

Exercise 5

When Martin went to put his name down for skiing lessons, he had this
conversation with the man at the ski centre.

MAN Good evening. Can I help you?

MARTIN Yes, I'd like to join a skiing class, if I can.

MAN Yes, it's possible. Have you done any skiing before?

MARTIN   No, I'm afraid I haven't.

MAN   It doesn't matter. You'll need to join a beginners' class. There's one on Wednesday evenings that isn't full.

MARTIN   Good. What time does it begin?

MAN   It begins at half-past seven and finishes at half-past eight. You can start next Wednesday.

MARTIN   Good. Do I have to pay anything now?

MAN   No, you needn't. Pay on Wednesday when you start. Goodbye.

Write more conversation like that for people joining a tennis club, a swimming club, an English class, a dancing class, a water-skiing class, a driving school and a flying school.

Exercise 6

When Jillian goes skiing, she needn't take her own skis, but she must take some money. Now put the words given in the right places.

When you go to play football you needn't take a — but you must take your own — . (pair of boots, football)

When you travel by plane you needn't take any — but you must have a — . (ticket, money)

To make coffee you needn't have — but you must have — . (water, milk)

An English — must go to school, but an English — needn't go to evening school. (woman, girl)

A — needn't buy petrol, but a — must. (man riding a bicycle, man driving a scooter)

A — needn't carry a light, but a — must. (car driving at night, man walking in the dark)

In England when you post a letter, you needn't write your own address on the — of the envelope, but you must put the address of the person you are writing to on the — . (front, back)

20

Exercise 7

Finish these sentences, using either "mustn't" or "needn't".

A boxer — always hit his man on the chin, but he — ever hit him below the belt.

In a public library you — borrow more than four books at the same time, but you — take four out if you don't want to.

When you are putting petrol in a car, you — always fill it full of petrol, but you — ever fill it too full.

The barman in an English pub — sell you drink after closing-time, and he — sell you it before that if you have already drunk too much.

When the traffic lights are red, people in cars — go past, but people on foot — wait.

Exercise 8

Practise with a friend asking politely for things.

Ask for the time, your friend's name, your friend's address, the date, your friend's job. (Would you mind telling me — .)

Ask where places are. Ask for the nearest cinema, post-box, record shop, hospital, church. (Would you mind showing me — .)

Pretend you are at the dinner table. Ask for the salt, another spoon, a glass, some butter, the bread basket. (Would you mind passing — . Friend: Certainly, here you are.)

Pretend you are in a cinema. Tell your friend not to sit on your hat, not to sing during the film, not to eat fruit in the cinema, not to take his shoes off, not to stand on your foot. (Would you mind not sitting (etc.) — . Friend: Oh, certainly. I'm very sorry.)

Exercise 9

What can you remember? Don't read the story, but try to remember who said these sentences, and who they were speaking to.

I began learning to ski when I was twelve.
Would you mind giving me a few skiing lessons?
I can't put off telling you any longer.
You must think about keeping your feet together.

20

Who did these things, and what else were they doing at the time?

Who remembered hearing somebody talking about an artificial ski slope in London?
Who said somebody was playing about at the bottom of the slope?
Who kept on laughing and laughing?
Who started desperately to explain?

Exercise 10   Conversation practice

A | I | like walking
love going | past your garden. It's so | pretty. beautiful.

B | Oh, thank you.
I'm glad you like it.

A | Your flowers are still | there living | when | everybody else's other people's

have | gone. died.

B | Yes, I'm | quite very | lucky, aren't I?

A | Would you mind telling me why they never die?
What's your way of stopping them from dying?

B | Don't tell anybody, will you?
Please keep my secret, won't you? | They're all | artificial. made of plastic.

Unit 21

He started to shout
He started shouting

Martin likes to smoke a pipe.	He likes smoking a pipe.
He started to smoke when he was 21.	He started smoking when he was 21.
He began to ski in Unit 20.	He began skiing in Unit 20.
He likes to ski.	He likes skiing.
Jill loves to ski, too.	Jill loves skiing, too.

Exercise 1

Look at the photographs again.

1
*My first long
trousers. Age 12.*

2
*At the swimming
pool. Age 8.*

3
*After my first driving
lesson. Age 17.*

4
*An early walk
with Jill. Age 20.*

5
*My first car.
Age 21.*

6
*In the mountains.
Age 21.*

Ask somebody to answer these questions, using "to — ".

When did Martin start to wear long trousers?
Do boys like to wear long trousers?
When did Martin start to have swimming lessons?
Did he like to go swimming then?
When did he begin to have driving lessons?
Did his instructor like to have Martin with him?
When did Martin begin to go out with Jillian?
Did she like to go walking with him?
When did Martin start to take her out in his own car?
Did he love to have a car of his own?

Now ask the questions again, but use "–ing" instead of "to — ". Like
this: When did Martin start wearing long trousers?
Ask somebody to answer, using "–ing".

Exercise 2

How many true sentences can you make?

I	started began	learning to learn	to read to swim English	when I was —	years months	old.
		walking to walk talking to talk				

I didn't	start begin	learning to learn	to drive to dance music	until I was — years old.
		working to work studying to study		

He remembered to go

"Remember to write."
"Don't forget to write."

Exercise 3

In the picture on page 204, the twins were going away for a holiday and Martin was telling them what to do. He told them to put their tickets in their pockets, to get out at the right station, to be polite, to clean their shoes every day and to wash their ears.

Say ten sentences that Martin might have said, five beginning "Remember to — " and five beginning "Don't forget to — ."

Then say ten sentences that the boys might have said to each other, five beginning, "We must remember to — " and five beginning "We mustn't forget to — ."

He remembered going

Jillian remembers some things and forgets others.
Thinking about her wedding, she says:

Wearing my wedding dress was fun. I remember wearing my wedding dress.
Getting married in the church was awful. I don't remember getting married.
Cutting the wedding cake was difficult. I'll never forget cutting the wedding cake.
Martin says I hid from him in the Paris hotel. I don't remember hiding from him.

Exercise 4

Think back and say whether you remember or don't remember:

seeing a picture of Jillian wearing skis
seeing a picture of Martin in the park
seeing a picture of Jillian in a phone box
seeing a picture of Martin's middle-aged aunt
seeing a picture of Martin having a shower
reading about Jillian sunbathing
reading about Jillian getting a new job
reading about Martin using a launderette
thinking Jillian was very careless
wanting to stop studying English

Exercise 5

Write out these broken sentences correctly.

When you go to another country you must remember	meeting my best friend for the first time.
Until the day I die, I'll never forget	doing the things I didn't like.
Jillian sometimes forgets	to drive on the left side of the road.
When I think back, I usually forget	going to school the first time, because he didn't like it.
English car drivers must always remember	to take your passport with you.
Once when Jillian made a cake she forgot	to do the things she doesn't like.
Martin has never forgotten	losing it.
If you ever lose all your money, you'll never forget	being unkind, but remember when other people are unkind.
People who borrow things and forget	to switch the oven on.
People often don't remember	to give them back, often lose their friends.

21

House for sale

"Yes," said Martin's Aunt Myra, sighing, "I remember making plans to get married. I began looking round furniture shops and my young man began to look for somewhere to live. But then one day I saw him going out with another girl, and that was the end." She started to feel for a handkerchief, and Jillian jumped up from her armchair to take Aunt Myra's cup and saucer.

"Let me give you some more coffee," Jillian said, trying to change the subject, and looking desperately at Martin. But Aunt Myra shook her head. "No thank you dear. I must be going now. But I've been looking forward to seeing this flat and it was very kind of you two to ask me to come. Oh, there's something I almost forgot to say. Soon you might start thinking about buying a house."

Martin gave a short laugh. "We'd like to have a house of our own, but. . . ."

"Just a minute," Aunt Myra said, holding up a hand. "I'll never forget seeing the expression on my young man's face when he found we couldn't afford to buy a house. I don't want you two to be unhappy, and I want you to promise you'll start looking round for a house of your own. I've got a little money and you may borrow as much as you like."

Jillian and Martin started to thank her, but she left without another word. Through the window, Martin watched her walk away and then he turned to Jillian. "It's not a bad idea, darling," he said. "We needn't think of buying a house this year, but we can start to look at houses and try to find out how much nice ones cost."

"Yes," Jillian answered. "I remember seeing an advertisement for some new houses that are going up on the edge of the park. There's a show house open. Let's go and see whether it's still open."

As they walked round to the show house, Martin said "We'll have to do this seriously. We must remember to make sure how many rooms there are. I'll try to remember to see how big the garden is."

"And I'll remember to ask about the price," Jillian said. "This is going to be fun. You know, darling, we ought to stop spending so much money and start saving up. Let's stop going to our skiing lessons and stop giving parties."

"All right," Martin said. "We'll start putting more money in the bank, and instead of skiing and parties, we'll try to look at two new houses each week. Then when we've found the house we like, we can go and talk to Aunt Myra."

In that part of London near their flat there were many new houses for sale. And for several weeks they spent their free time looking round show houses. Sometimes as they went into a house Jillian whispered, "Don't forget to count the number of electric plugs in the kitchen," or "Try standing up in the cupboard under the stairs." After looking round other houses, Martin sometimes asked, "Do you remember hearing any traffic when we were in the living-room?" or "Did you remember to notice the colour of the lavatory?"

After six weeks they had looked round fourteen houses and had saved up only twelve pounds in the bank. "I'm afraid saving up for a house takes a long time," Jillian said, sighing. "I like going round all these houses, Martin, but I'm starting to get quite tired."

"Yes, I know," he answered. "Let's do something different this week-end. There are some very expensive houses for sale that we shall never be able to afford. Let's go and look at them, just to see the difference. They're not far from Aunt Myra's, but we needn't go and see her."

21

So the following Saturday afternoon, having remembered to put on their smartest clothes, Martin and Jillian drove round to the biggest and most modern show house they had ever visited.

"I don't remember seeing anything like this before," Jillian whispered, and Martin laughed, "No, and I don't remember seeing a price as high as that before. Look, it's £20,000. Come on, let's go in."

They started to walk round the house, trying to pretend they could afford it. Jillian tried opening all the doors of the expensive cupboards in the kitchen; Martin tried turning on all the taps in the two bathrooms.

"Don't forget to look at the garage, Martin," Jillian called, "there's room for two cars."

"Stop talking so loudly, darling," he answered, "you're getting excited."

At last, having finished looking round the expensive house, they came out laughing and talking like a couple of children.

"It's only twenty thousand, darling," Martin said in fun. "Shall we try looking at other houses, or would you like to have this one?"

"Oh this one, please," Jillian answered, laughing, "we can obviously stop looking at show houses now. And I would hate to live in a small house after seeing this one."

All at once a voice behind them said, "I thought you two hadn't got any money." It was Aunt Myra. "If you can afford to buy an expensive house like this, you don't need to borrow anything from me. Goodbye."

They watched her walking away, her head in the air. "I think, darling," Jillian said slowly, "I would like to have a party. If we're quick we can get to the wineshop before it closes."

It was later that week that Martin saw his father, who said, "I heard your Aunt Myra talking about you and Jillian. I don't know what she's been saying to you, but there's something I ought to tell you. She likes helping people and she likes to pretend she's got a lot of money. But she hasn't a penny in the world. And she never had a boy-friend."

Martin burst out laughing. "Poor Aunt Myra! What a pity! We must remember to ask her to come and visit us again."

New words

for sale, furniture, dear, almost, to thank, an edge, a show house, whether, to save up, all right, a bank, to whisper, modern, a thousand, a couple, room, to hate, penny, poor.

Exercise 6

Talk about the book you are reading at the moment.

I	began started	it reading it to read it	(*when?*)

I	shall finish hope to finish think I shall finish	it reading it	(*when?*)

I	like love hate	to read reading	it	(*where?*)

Now talk about something you are doing or planning to do.

I	began started	it doing it to do it planning to do it to plan to do it	(*when?*)

I	shall finish hope to finish think I shall finish	it doing it planning it	(*when?*)

Now talk in the same way about your job and say why you like or hate it.

Exercise 7

Read the story again before answering these questions.

Why did Aunt Myra start feeling for her handkerchief?
What was Martin starting to say when Aunt Myra stopped him?

21

Had Martin and Jillian started saving up for their own house before Aunt
  Myra's visit?
Why do you think Jillian wanted to count electric plugs?
Why did Martin try to remember hearing traffic in the living-room?
Why, when visiting the expensive house, did they wear their smartest
  clothes?
Why did Jillian begin to get excited?
What did Jillian mean when she said they could stop looking at show
  houses?
What did Aunt Myra think when she met Jillian and Martin outside the
  £20,000 house?
Why did Jillian start wanting to have parties again?

Exercise 8
You will never forget some things. Write ten sentences starting:

I'll	never forget always remember	seeing hearing going to meeting buying	— .

Exercise 9
Finish these sentences, using either "–ing" or "to — ". Try to make true
sentences.

I remember — .
I started — .
I went — .
I'm looking forward to — .
I tried — .
I'm learning — .
I've stopped — .
I like practising — .
I'll never forget beginning — .
Would you mind — .

I forgot — .
I hate — .
I'm thinking of — .
I like — .
I love — .
I would like — .
I'm planning — .
I don't feel like — .
I want to try — .
I must remember — .

21

Exercise 10   Conversation practice

Pretend you are in a restaurant. The waiter and the customer are both polite.

CUSTOMER   Excuse me, waiter.

WAITER   Yes sir?

CUSTOMER   I'm afraid this fish is quite cold.

WAITER   Oh, I'm very sorry, sir.

CUSTOMER   Would you mind taking it back to the kitchen, please.

WAITER   Certainly, sir. I'll try to make sure it doesn't happen again.

This time both the waiter and the customer are impolite.

CUSTOMER   Hey you!

WAITER   What do you want?

CUSTOMER   I hate eating cold fish. This is horrible.

WAITER   It's not my fault.

CUSTOMER   Well, take it away.

WAITER   If you don't like our food, you needn't come here.

Now practise again, with a polite waiter and an impolite customer. Then with a polite customer and an impolite waiter.

Unit 22

He wanted to go
He wanted me to go

Martin shouted for one of the boys.
Tim wanted to stay. He didn't want to go.
Tony wanted to stay. He didn't want to go.
Martin asked one of them to help him.
Tim told Tony to go.
Tony told Tim to go.

Exercise 1

As you know, Tom works on a newspaper. Sometimes there are funny
drawings in his paper – cartoons. But when the artist has drawn a cartoon,

he often can't decide what words to write underneath. Here are two cartoons, but there are several sentences with each. Say which sentence you think Tom used. And decide who is talking.

"I've always wanted to have a
  ship of my own."
"I promised to buy you a
  present."
"Now you can pretend to be
  captain."
"I couldn't afford to buy
  anything bigger."
"But I've decided to be a plane
  pilot."
"I know I said I wanted to feel
  younger, but. . . ."

"We're getting ready to clean
  the windows."
"He's promised to stop using the
  lift."
"When are they planning to put
  your stairs in?"
"We're hoping to give our
  friends a surprise."
"Why do you need to have a
  longer washing line?"
"He wants to use his new
  climbing rope."

Exercise 2
Look at the two cartoons in Exercise 1 again, then read these ten new sentences. Say which cartoon each sentence goes with, and decide who is speaking. Then decide which two sentences Tom used.

"The doctor told him to stop climbing stairs."
"I couldn't get him to take an interest in me."
"Ask your captain to let you have a bath more often."
"Tell him to remember his key another time."
"She wanted us to have something to talk about."

"It will help you to keep your mind on your work."
"But why doesn't her father want her to marry a climber?"
"It's the only way you'll get me to take you to the park."
"He asked me to go sunbathing with him on the roof."
"Her father told him to stop knocking on their door."

Exercise 3
How many true sentences can you make? Write five.

When I	want need am getting ready am hoping have decided am planning	to go	shopping on holiday	I	ask get tell

a friend somebody	to	lend me some money. show me the best places.

He knows where to go
He asked me where to go

I don't know where to take him.
I can't think what to do with him.
Do you know how to talk to him?
We must find out when to give him food.

Ask somebody where to take him.
Who can tell us what to do with him?
Who can show us how to talk to him?
Perhaps he'll tell us when to give him food.

Exercise 4

Sometimes when it is difficult to decide what to do, we ask our friends.
Read these sentences, then ask a friend what to do.
Like this:
You are going to a party, but you don't know what to wear.
Say to your friend, "I'm going to a party. Can you tell me what to wear?"

You want to buy your mother a present, but you can't decide what to buy
   her.
An Englishman has asked you to go to his house, but you are wondering
   when to arrive.
Somebody is meeting you outside the cinema, but you are not sure how
   to get there.
You are looking for a petrol station, but you don't know where to find one.
You have found a wallet, but you are wondering who to take it to.
You've got two books by the same writer, but you need to know which to
   read first.
Another friend has given you two telephone numbers, but you are not
   sure which to ring during the day.
Somebody has been impolite to you and you don't know what to do about
   it.
You want to save up some money, but you are wondering where to keep it.
You want to visit England during the warm weather, so you want to
   know when to go.

Exercise 5

Practise finding the way to places. (Get your friends to try to give sensible
answers.) Tell them:

I'm	looking for / trying to find	a / the	petrol station / bus station / railway station	post office / football club / bank	show house / town square / law court / college

	but	I don't know / I'm wondering / I'm trying to find out	how to get there. / where to go. / what to do. / which way to go.

Now ask for the same places in another way.

Please	tell show	me	how to get to where to find	—
Would you mind	telling showing	me	what to do to get to which way to go for	

Tom's fish

Tom rang the doorbell of Martin and Jillian's flat one Sunday afternoon and, wearing a broad smile, came in with a long parcel.

"I promised to bring you one," he said, "and here I am."

"Well, come in," Jillian answered, wondering what he was talking about.

"I want to show you two I'm a better fisherman than you think."

"Ah," said Martin, beginning to understand. He remembered Tom saying he was going to go fishing, and Tom had promised to bring them a fish.

"I'm afraid I can't stay," Tom went on loudly, "but here it is." He started opening his parcel and took out a large salmon.

"But it's huge!" Jillian exclaimed. "We can't hope to eat all that."

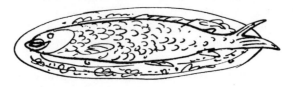

"Then get somebody to help you," Tom answered, laughing. "I see you've got a cat. Give some to him."

"Yes," Martin said, looking down at the cat that was rubbing itself against his legs. "Peter brought it round last night and asked us to give it a home."

"Salmon's too good for a cat," Jillian said. "This is a marvellous fish. Thanks a lot, Tom."

They heard him drive away noisily on his motor cycle, and stood, looking at the huge salmon and wondering what to do.

"Do you know how to cook it?" Martin asked, then realized too late he had said the wrong thing.

"I can soon find out what to do," Jillian answered coldly. "I've got my picture cookery book that shows you how to cook everything. Do you know what wine to drink with salmon?"

But before he could think what to say, Jillian had an idea. "Listen, there's far too much fish here for us. Let's ask Peter and Liz to come and share it."

"What a good idea!" Martin said. "I'll ring them now. You go and start getting ready to cook it and I'll come and help you to do things in a minute."

He came back a few minutes later, smiling. "I've persuaded them to come. They wanted to know what time to arrive, so I told them to be here about eight. Now tell me what to do to help you."

"Just leave me alone, please dear," she answered, pretending to read her cookery book. "You go round the wine shop and find out what to drink with salmon." She waited until she heard Martin going out of the front door, then rushed to the telephone to ask her mother how to cook a huge fish.

At half past seven they were almost ready. The knives and forks shone on the table, the wine and wineglasses, the plates and dishes were all ready, and Jillian and Martin stood for a moment looking proudly at the salmon lying on a large dish on a little table at the side. They smiled at each other, then went into their bedroom to get ready.

"I've decided to wear my new dress," Jillian said.

"You're a super cook, darling," Martin whispered.

"Well, you're learning to be very helpful," she laughed. And they kissed.

Coming into the living-room two minutes later, they found the cat on the little table with the salmon, a large piece of fish in its mouth.

22

"The fish!" Martin exclaimed, rushing to the cat. He picked it up and put it quickly out of the front door. "I think I saw Peter's car coming," he called, as Jillian came out of the kitchen carrying the salmon.

"It's all right," she said, "I've cut a piece out of the fish where the cat had been eating. They needn't know." And at that moment the doorbell started ringing.

"That was super," Liz said, looking at her empty plate.

"Yes, you've got a clever wife, Martin," Peter said.

"And there's just a little fish left for the cat," Jillian laughed, looking secretly at Martin, who didn't know where to look.

"Yes, I'll go and see where he is," Martin said, getting up from the table and going to the front door. He opened it and looking down, saw the cat lying dead on the doorstep. As he picked it up gently he remembered the cat eating the salmon. "And we've all had some, too," he thought, suddenly feeling ill.

"The cat's dead," he said quietly to the others. They were silent.

Then Jillian said, quickly, "Liz, Peter, there's something we ought to tell you. We found the cat eating some of the salmon before you came. And now . . . he's dead."

"I don't feel very well," Martin said.

"Nor do I," Liz whispered, and the colour started to leave her cheeks.

Jillian ran towards the bathroom door, calling, "Ring the doctor, Martin. Quickly. Ask him what to do."

As Martin went to the telephone, it began to ring. It was Tom at the other end.

"I say, Martin," he said. "I'm terribly sorry. Have you found out?"

"What?" Martin asked in a low voice.

"Well, I was driving past your flat an hour ago on my motor cycle," he said, "and I'm afraid I hit your poor cat. It died at once. But I didn't want to spoil your evening, so I put the cat on your doorstep. I'm awfully sorry."

"Don't worry, Tom." Martin answered, feeling better already. "It wasn't your fault I'm sure. Oh – and I mustn't forget to thank you for the salmon. It was excellent. Goodbye."

New words

a parcel, a salmon, huge, to exclaim, to rub, a motor cycle, to cook, coldly, cookery, to persuade, alone, a dish, proudly, a cook, dead, a doorstep, to spoil, excellent.

Exercise 6
Read the story again and then answer these questions:

Why did Tom bring Jillian and Martin the salmon?
Why did Jillian exclaim when she first saw it?
Why do you think the cat started rubbing itself against Martin's leg?
Why did Martin think he had said the wrong thing to Jillian?
Why did Jillian speak coldly?
Why did she tell Martin to leave her alone?
Why did Jillian and Martin look proudly at the salmon?
Why did Jillian take the salmon back into the kitchen?
Why did Martin think the cat had died?
Why did Jillian explain quickly to Peter and Liz about the cat eating the fish?
Why did Martin start to feel ill?
Why did Jillian ask him to phone the doctor?
Why did Tom ring up?
Why hadn't he brought the cat in after he had hit it?
Why did Martin start to feel better?

Exercise 7
Ask somebody:

Did Jillian know how to cook a salmon?
Where did she try to find out how to cook it?
Did Martin know what to drink with the salmon?
Where did he find out what to drink with it?
Who wanted to know when to arrive?
Who told them when to arrive?
When did Jillian decide what to wear?
When and why didn't Martin know where to look?
How did Martin know where to find the cat?
Why didn't Martin ask the doctor what to do?

22

Exercise 8

Put ten sensible questions to your friends using the following verbs.

to afford, to decide, to get ready, to hope, to learn, to need, to plan, to pretend, to promise, to want.

Make sure that in every sentence you use "to — " after the verb. Like this: When you can't afford to buy something you want, what do you do?

Now ask six more sensible questions using the following verbs.
to ask, to get, to help, to persuade, to tell, to want.

Make sure that in every sentence you use "somebody to — " after the verb. Like this: When you ask somebody to tell you the time, what do you say?
Your friends must give sensible answers.

Exercise 9

Ask ten sensible questions using the following verbs.

to decide, to explain, to find out, to know, to learn, to plan, to talk about, to think, to understand, to wonder.

Make sure that in every sentence you use the verb, then a "wh–" word (what, when, where, which, who or how) and then "to —". For example: Have you decided what to do tomorrow evening?

Now ask four more sensible questions using the following verbs.

to ask, to show, to teach, to tell.

Make sure that in every sentence you use the verb, then somebody, then a "wh–" word and then "to —". For example: Have you asked anybody where to take your broken watch?

22

Exercise 10   A telephone conversation

Here are three conversations between a secretary and somebody calling
on the telephone. In the first conversation both are polite, in the second
they are less polite and in the third, they are both impolite. Practise
several times, changing the way the two people speak to each other.

SECRETARY   Good afternoon. Can I help you?

CALLER   Do you think I might speak to the manager please?

SECRETARY   I'm afraid he's not in the office at the moment. Would
you like me to try to get his assistant?

CALLER   No, it's not important, thank you. I'll try to phone again
tomorrow. Goodbye.

SECRETARY   Goodbye, sir.

SECRETARY   Yes?

CALLER   I want to speak to the manager.

SECRETARY   He's not here at the moment. Shall I try to get his
assistant?

CALLER   No, it doesn't matter. I'll ring again tomorrow. Goodbye.

SECRETARY   Goodbye.

SECRETARY   Well?

CALLER   Give me the manager.

SECRETARY   He's not in. Do you want his assistant?

CALLER   No, that's no good. Goodbye.

SECRETARY   Goodbye!

Unit 23

He used to swim

Martin doesn't go to school now, but he used to go.
He used to learn French and German.
He used to study geography and history.
He used to have science and mathematics lessons.
He used to play football at school, too.

Exercise 1
Here is the timetable from Martin's old school.

M	Maths	Maths	English	Music	French	History	German
T	English	Geog.	German	English	French	Science	Science
W	Maths	Maths	English	French	Games		
Th	English	Geog.	German	History	Music	Science	Science
F	Maths	Maths	Library	English	French	History	German

How many sentences can you make?

Martin Martin's class He They	used to	do have study learn	French German English history	geography maths science music
		play football		

on	Monday. Tuesday. Wednesday. Thursday. Friday.

23

Did he use to swim?

Exercise 2
Look at the school timetable again and ask questions.

When How often	did they use to	do have study learn	French? German? English? history?	geography? maths? science? music?
		play football?		

He didn't use to swim

Exercise 3
Looking again at Martin's timetable, how many true sentences can you make?

Martin Martin's class He They	didn't use to	do have study learn	French German English history	geography maths science music	on	Mondays. Tuesdays. Wednesdays. Thursdays. Fridays.
		play football				

Exercise 4
Think back to the time when you were a child, and answer these questions.

Did you use to go to school, church, the cinema, swimming, football matches?
Did you use to listen to music, concerts, pop records, the radio?
Did you use to play football, tennis, cricket, quiet games, noisy games?
Did you use to have a cat, a dog, a particular friend, a lot of homework?

23

At the waxworks exhibition

One rainy Saturday afternoon, Jillian and Martin were wondering what to do, when suddenly Martin had an idea.

"I know," he said enthusiastically, "I'll take you to a place my father used to take me to when I was a boy. No, don't ask questions; just get your umbrella and get into the car."

Half an hour later they stopped outside a large building and Jillian laughed.

"Oh, it's the waxworks exhibition. Do you know, I've never been before?"

And Martin said, "Oh, we used to come here often when I was little. There used to be a lot of famous people inside, all made of wax, but I suppose they've changed most of them now."

While Martin was buying the tickets at the pay-desk, Jillian looked round.

"Did your mother use to come too?" she asked.

"Not very often," Martin told her. "She used to stay at home and look after Susan and the twins, who were babies then. Come on, up these stairs."

At the top of the stairs stood an attendant, holding some catalogues. Jillian went up to her, opening her handbag, while Martin watched her.

"How much are the catalogues, please?" Jillian asked, but the girl didn't answer. And she didn't realise that she had been talking to a wax-work until she heard Martin laughing behind her.

"There used to be a waxwork policeman near the entrance and people used to go and ask him the time," he said. "Come on."

Although it was a Saturday afternoon, the exhibition halls were not full of people. So Jillian and Martin could walk round comfortably. They stopped to look at a group of politicians.

"Times change, don't they?" Martin said. "These chaps didn't use to be here ten years ago." Then he started to laugh. "I've just remembered, darling. I sometimes used to come here with a friend and while nobody was looking, we used to change the names of the waxworks. The attendants didn't use to think it was funny, but we did."

While Martin was speaking, Jillian had been watching one of the attendants, standing behind him. He was a little old man with a moustache and thick glasses. He hadn't moved at all and although Jillian had watched him all the time Martin was speaking, she hadn't seen him

23

blink. "Yes," she told herself, "he's a waxwork, too." And she thought she would play a trick on Martin. So, when he wasn't looking, she hung the handle of her umbrella over the attendant's wrist, and walked away quickly.

A few minutes later, having arrived in another part of the exhibition, Jillian turned to Martin and said, "Oh, darling, I've left my umbrella behind. I gave it to an attendant to look after, the one with a moustache in the politicians' room. Would you mind going for it?"

Martin smiled to himself as he went back to the other room. "She wants me to start a conversation with a waxwork," he thought. So when he saw Jillian's umbrella on the attendant's wrist where she had hung it, he went straight up to the man and took hold of the umbrella handle. But the attendant stopped him and said, "Excuse me, sir, but I don't think it's your umbrella." Martin was so surprised that the little old man was not a waxwork that he didn't know what to say.

"No, I know it's not mine," he began. "You see, I thought you were..."

Behind his glasses, the attendant's eyes shone. "I see, sir. You thought you would take this umbrella from me, because you thought I was part of the exhibition. Yes, there used to be a lot of people like you coming in." Then he looked closely at Martin. "Yes, you used to come here about ten years ago with a friend, didn't you? You used to change the names of the waxworks, didn't you? You thought nobody saw you, didn't you?"

226

23

By this time, Martin was blushing bright red and he turned round to see Jillian, who had heard the last part of the conversation. She laughed, went up to the attendant and said, "May I have my umbrella now, please? I knew you would look after it for me." The little old man passed it to her with a smile.

As they were leaving the building, Martin said faintly, "But he remembered seeing me in there ten years ago. He remembered my face. Oh this is awful. I shall have to grow a moustache or a beard, or dye my hair or something. But how could he remember seeing me ten years ago?"

When they were in the car, Jillian said, "You know, that attendant heard you telling me about what you used to do when you were a boy. He was only pretending to remember seeing you ten years ago. I think he was just playing a trick on us for thinking he was a waxwork."

"I suppose so," Martin answered, but he was not quite sure.

New words

waxworks, an exhibition, an umbrella, a building, wax, to suppose, an attendant, a catalogue, although, to blink, a trick, to hang, a handle, a wrist, straight, to blush, bright, to grow, a beard, to dye.

Exercise 5

In the story, Jillian thought she would play a trick on Martin. To herself she said, "I will play a trick on Martin."

Now read these sentences and write down what the people said to themselves.

Martin thought he would take Jillian to the waxworks exhibition.
He knew she would like it.
He knew a lot of the old waxworks would have disappeared.
Jillian thought she would buy a catalogue.
Martin knew the girl attendant wouldn't sell her one.
Jillian thought the old man would blink if he wasn't made of wax.
She decided she would put her umbrella on his wrist.
Martin said he would go and get Jillian's umbrella.
Martin decided he would have to grow a beard.

23

Exercise 6
Read the story again, then answer these questions.

What did Jillian think the attendant with the catalogues was doing?
Did Martin know it was a waxwork girl?
How do you think Martin and his friend could change the names?
Why did Jillian suppose the little old man was made of wax?
What did Martin think when he went for Jillian's umbrella?
What was Martin going to say to the attendant?
Why do you think the attendant had heard Martin telling Jillian about changing the names?
Why did the old attendant pretend to remember Martin?
Why did Martin blush?
Why did Martin say he ought to grow a beard or a moustache?

Exercise 7
Finish these sentences using one of the following: as, when, while, although, until.

Jillian didn't visit the waxworks exhibition — after she got married.
She didn't know where she was going — they arrived.
Martin's mother looked after the babies — his father took him to the waxworks.
Martin watched Jillian — she tried to buy a catalogue.
— the policeman was inside the waxworks exhibition, people tried to talk to him.
Martin and Jillian could walk round comfortably — it was a wet Saturday afternoon.
— Martin was talking, Jillian watched the little old man.
— Martin went back for the umbrella, he smiled to himself.
The attendant said nothing — Martin tried to take the umbrella.
Martin saw the attendant's eyes shine — he wore glasses.
— the old man was speaking, Martin's face was growing redder.
— he was speaking, Jillian arrived.
The attendant smiled — he passed the umbrella to Jillian.
Jillian explained what had happened — they had got into the car.
— Jillian explained this, Martin was not quite sure what to think.

228

23

Exercise 8

When Martin was at school he used to do exercises like this.
Find the word that doesn't go with the others in the group, e.g.

window   wall   glass   look through   fish

The answer is "fish" because you don't usually think of fish when you
hear "window". Now do the same with these:

wrist	hand	arm	detective	watch
banana	fruit	fur	yellow	tree
boot	foot	car	shoe	flour
cinema	collar	film	queue	ticket
beard	man	hair	face	tap
salmon	red	dangerous	fish	food
motorcycle	meat	petrol	fast	noisy
furniture	house	flowers	chair	bed
whisper	winter	quiet	secret	voice
shut	close	open	loud	eyes

Exercise 9

Ask somebody:

Are you as — * as you used to be? *or* Did you use to be as — * as you
are now?

* heavy, light, big, small, strong, weak, rich, poor, happy, unhappy.

Perhaps the answer will be: I didn't use to be as heavy (etc.) as I am
now. *or* I used to be heavier (etc.) than I am now.

23

Exercise 10   Conversation practice

Martin bought his tickets from the girl in the pay-desk. Practise this conversation between a man buying tickets for an exhibition and the girl at the ticket office. They are both speaking formally.

VISITOR   Good afternoon.

GIRL   Good afternoon, sir.

VISITOR   What is the price of entrance, please?

GIRL   Ten pence per head, sir.

VISITOR   Then let me have two tickets, please.

GIRL   Certainly, sir. Here are your tickets.

VISITOR   Thank you very much.

Now practise this different conversation between a man going into a dance hall and the girl selling tickets. They are both speaking informally.

VISITOR   Hello.

GIRL   Hello.

VISITOR   How much does it cost to go in?

GIRL   Ten pence each.

VISITOR   I'll have two, then.

GIRL   Here you are.

VISITOR   Thanks.

Now make a conversation between a formal man buying a ticket from an informal girl at a football ground ticket office.

Then make another conversation between an informal man going into a concert and a formal girl selling the tickets.

Unit 24

He will be writing

Martin's boss, who is a designer, is going to visit several countries and has asked Martin to book his tickets at a travel agent's. This is the list Martin gave him.

Sunday 12th fly to Brussels.
Tuesday 14th train to Paris.
Friday 17th fly to Geneva.
Sunday 19th fly to Rome.
Wednesday 22nd fly to Vienna.
Friday 24th train to Munich.
Sunday 26th fly to London.

Martin gave him this timetable and said, "You'll be travelling on these dates. On the other dates you'll be meeting people."

Exercise 1
Look at the timetable and make true sentences.

He will be	flying to travelling to arriving in leaving staying in	Brussels Paris Geneva Rome Vienna Munich London	on — .

Will he be writing?

Exercise 2
Pretend you are Martin and answer your boss's questions.

Shall I be visiting Austria before or after Italy?
Shall I be going to France before or after Switzerland?
When shall I be travelling by plane?
When shall I be travelling by train?
Where shall I be staying the longest?

What shall I be doing on the two Saturdays I am away?
How long shall I be staying in France and Germany?
What day of the week shall I be meeting people in Vienna?

He said, "He will be writing"
He said he would be writing

Martin told his boss he would be travelling on those dates. He told him he would be meeting people on other dates.

Exercise 3
How many true sentences can you make? Write ten.

Martin	told him said	he would be	flying to travelling to arriving in leaving staying in	Brussels Paris Geneva Rome Vienna Munich London	on — .

Exercise 4
Tell somebody what Martin's boss wanted to know in Exercise 2.
For example, he asked Martin if he would be visiting Austria before or after Italy.
Then tell somebody how Martin answered.
For example, I told him he would be visiting Austria after Italy.

On the underground

Jillian's boss at the B.B.C. called her into his office one morning and said, "Jill, would you mind doing something for me? You know there are some new furniture designs I shall be talking about in the programme this afternoon. They haven't arrived. I've just phoned through to the design office and they're sending somebody with them. But would you mind going to meet him, to save time? Go to the entrance hall of Baker

Street underground station and the young man will be waiting there. You'll recognize him because he'll be carrying a large envelope of designs. Bring them straight back to me in the studio – I'll be rehearsing the programme by that time."

Jillian arrived at the Baker Street underground entrance hall and started to watch the crowds going by. But there was no young man carrying a large envelope.

"I knew he wouldn't be waiting for me," she said to herself, looking at her watch. "And they'll be starting to rehearse the programme in a minute. Perhaps I had better get my return ticket while I'm waiting."

But as she stood at the ticket machine, she saw somebody that made her forget the young man from the design office. Martin, carrying his briefcase, was coming up the escalator towards her. She was going to run to him, when she stopped herself. That young man would be coming any minute, she thought. And what would Martin say if he saw her there with another man? He used to be jealous. She needn't talk to him now; she would be seeing him at tea-time and there would be time to explain then. So she turned her back on the escalator and stood still.

Suddenly she realized what was happening. "Why am I hiding from my own husband?" she thought. "I wonder what I shall be thinking of next." As she turned round, Martin's head and shoulders were just

disappearing as he went back down the other escalator.

"Now why has he come up one escalator and gone straight down another?" she wondered. "Perhaps he doesn't want me to see him."

"Oh damn this young man from the design office," she said between her teeth. She took a quick look round the entrance hall, but nobody was standing waiting. "Martin will be down on the platform waiting for a train," she thought. "I've got time to go down the escalator and have a word with him. Then perhaps this young man will be waiting with his envelope when I come back again."

The two escalators were side by side, and as Jillian was moving down on hers, she watched the people coming up on the other. She was nearly halfway down when she saw Martin coming up again on her left.

"What are you doing here?" he called, as he came closer. Jillian turned round and started running up the stairs while the escalator kept on moving downwards. Martin started running down his escalator as it moved upwards.

"I can't stop," Jillian shouted. "I think somebody will be meeting me at the top. And my boss will be getting worried." She stopped running as she knocked against another passenger, and the escalator carried her downwards again.

"That's funny," Martin shouted, waving his briefcase as he disappeared upwards. "I thought somebody would be waiting for me, too." Just then somebody knocked against him and his briefcase fell out of his hand and started to slide down the division between the two escalators.

Jillian arrived breathless at the bottom, just in time to catch the briefcase. Quickly she jumped onto the other escalator that was going up and found Martin waiting for her at the top. He opened his briefcase anxiously and took out a large envelope.

"Oh good, darling, it's safe. You know," he said, looking round, "my boss said somebody would be meeting me here – somebody from the B.B.C." And as he spoke, they both realized what had happened. "You're the girl my boss said would be coming for the designs."

"And you're the young man my boss said would be bringing them."

Jillian looked at her watch as she took the envelope. "Oh dear, he'll be biting his nails," she said, "I'd better go straight away. Will you be coming home early, darling?"

"The usual time," he called, and went towards the down escalator.

"Ah, there you are. I was getting worried," Jillian's boss said, as she walked in breathlessly. "Have you got the designs? Was he a nice young man?"

"Oh, super," she answered coolly. "I shall be seeing a lot of him in the future."

New words

underground, a design, to save, to recognize, a studio, to rehearse, a crowd, I had better — , an escalator, a platform, downwards, upwards, to get worried, to knock against, to wave, to slide, a division, breathless, to bite, breathlessly, coolly.

24

Exercise 5

Jillian thought she had better get her return ticket early. Perhaps you often tell people what they had better do. Say "You had better . . .", making sensible answers to these things your friends might say.

I'm very tired.
I'm thirsty.
I feel ill.
I'd like a cigarette.
I don't like my job.
My hair needs washing.
I've no toothpaste.
I've left my umbrella behind and it's started to rain.

I'm hungry.
I haven't any money.
I feel quite breathless.
I've lost my way.
I've broken my shoelace.
I can never wake up in the mornings.
I've just had my tenth driving accident.

Exercise 6

Read the story again and answer these questions.

Who did Jill's boss say would be waiting for her at Baker Street underground station?
How did he say she would recognize him?
What did he say he would be doing when she came back?
When did Jillian think she would be seeing Martin?
Why did she ask herself what she would be thinking of next?
Where did Jillian think Martin would be waiting for a train?
Who did she think she would see when she came up the escalator again?
Why did Jillian think her boss would be getting worried?
Who did Martin think would be waiting for him in the underground station?
What did Jillian say her boss would be doing when he was worried?
When did Martin say he would be coming home?
Why did Jillian say she would be seeing a lot of the young man she had met?

Exercise 7

When Martin thinks about "pen", these words come into his mind:

pencil, ink, writing, ball-pen, pocket.

Write down the English words that come into your mind when you think of the following:

father, wheel, music, white, to swim, kettle, to travel, to bite, grass, dangerous.

Exercise 8

Ask somebody:

What will you be doing	tomorrow at this time? at midnight tonight? next year at this time? the next time we meet? on Sunday afternoon?

Answer: I shall be — .
Then tell somebody else: I said I should be — .

Exercise 9

Think about the story again.

Jillian went to meet Martin halfway between his office and the B.B.C. Did this help the designs to arrive there more quickly than if Martin had come all the way?

Jillian bought her return ticket early to save time. Was this a sensible idea?

You know why Jillian didn't go to Martin as soon as she saw him? Was she right?

Martin went down the escalator as soon as he had reached the top. Why do you think he did this?

How many times in the story did Jillian and Martin use the escalators? Explain why for each time.

Which of them ought to have realized first why the other was there? Why?

What do you think Jillian's boss thought when she said she would be seeing a lot of the young man in the future?

24

Exercise 10   Conversation practice

Practise this conversation between a driving instructor and a learner at the end of a lesson when everything has gone wrong. Practise it three times, with the instructor being patient (first line), then less patient (second line) and finally being impatient (third line).

INSTRUCTOR
{ Right! Would you mind stopping now, please.
Right! Stop now.
Stop.

LEARNER   There. How did I do?

INSTRUCTOR
{ Well, I'm afraid you're not the best driver I've seen.
Well, you're not a very good driver.
Well, you're a terrible driver.

LEARNER   Why do you say that?

INSTRUCTOR
{ There are one or two things you don't find easy.
You appear to have difficulty with most things.
You can't do anything right.

LEARNER   Oh dear! What do you think I ought to do?

INSTRUCTOR
{ Perhaps you ought not to try to drive.
You had better stop having lessons.
Walk.

Unit 25

He will have written

I haven't finished yet. But I've only
  two more pages to read.
I shall have finished in five
  minutes.
I've read all his other books and
  this is the last one.
When I've finished this, I shall have
  read all his books.

Exercise 1

Look back at the timetable that Martin made for his boss, at the beginning
of Unit 24. Pretend you are making the journey and ask:

Shall I have	arrived in left been to finished in	Belgium France Switzerland Italy Austria Germany	by the	12th? 17th? 22nd? 13th? 18th? 23rd? 14th? 19th? 24th? 15th? 20th? 25th? 16th? 21st? 26th?

Give Martin's answers.

No, you won't have	arrived in left	Belgium France Switzerland	until the	12th. 20th. 13th. 21st. 14th. 22nd. 15th. 23rd.
Yes, you will have	been to finished in	Italy Austria Germany	on the	16th. 24th. 17th. 25th. 18th. 26th. 19th.

He will have been writing

JILLIAN You started reading that book at two o'clock. When you finish you will have been reading for four hours.

MARTIN Yes, I started studying this man's books nearly five years ago. I shall soon have been reading him for five years.

Exercise 2

How many true sentences can you make?

Next	week month year	I shall have been	learning English living in my present house working in my present job living working

for —	days. weeks. months. years.

Then look at the three cars in the car park once again on page 241. Write five true sentences.

At	three o'clock a quarter past three half past three	the	first second third	car will have been

standing waiting	there for — .

Exercise 3

Practise this conversation:

A You will have been using my ballpoint pen for a month, next week.
B Yes, I've been using it a lot. Do you need it back?
A Well, will you have finished with it by Monday? I'd like to use it then.
B Yes, I'll certainly have finished with it by then. In fact, I've been waiting for you to ask for it back.

Now make up more conversations, but this time talk about an alarm clock, a record-player, a sewing machine, a stamp catalogue and an umbrella.

Rent or hire-purchase?

"Yes," said Martin's mother, looking across the room at Martin and Jillian, "we shall have been married twenty-five years next week. It's our silver wedding anniversary."

"Congratulations," Jillian said, politely. "And I hope you'll both still be sitting here for your golden wedding anniversary." They all laughed.

"You know," his father said, "I've decided we ought to have a new television for an anniversary present. There's nothing wrong with this one, although we shall have had it for three years next month. But next week's a rather special occasion. In fact, Martin, I knew you two would be coming this evening, and I thought I would ask you what to do. Shall we be saving more money if we rent a new television, than if we buy one on hire-purchase?"

Martin looked at the piece of paper his father passed him. It said:

HIRE-PURCHASE
Deposit: £17.
Payments: £2·50 per month for 24 months.

RENT
Deposit: £24 (12 months in advance).
Payments: £2 per month after the first year.

Jillian looked over Martin's shoulder. "If you rent a television, what will you have paid at the end of the first year?"

"Only the deposit," Martin answered.

"Yes," said his father. "I shall have paid only £24 after a year. But if I buy one on hire-purchase I shall have paid £47 after a year. It will cost much less to rent."

"Of course, it will," Jillian said. "If you are renting, you will have been paying less each month, but you won't have been buying your set. If you do it on hire-purchase, you will have bought your television at the end of two years. But you will never have bought your set, if you decide to rent one, although you will have been paying for it for several years."

25

Then Martin's mother joined in. "How much money shall we have spent at the end of two years renting?" she asked.

Martin looked at the paper. "At the end of two years you'll have spent £24 on the advance: then for the second year you will have been paying two pounds per month. So it will have cost you £48."

"But by hire-purchase," she said, waving a finger, "we shall have been paying two pounds fifty a month and we'll have been doing that for two years. At the end of two years we shall have spent £77."

"Yes," Martin said loudly. "But you'll have bought your own set. And at the end of five years, the person who rents will have paid £120. But on hire-purchase, you'll still only have spent £77."

Going home in the car, Martin said, "They'll still be talking about it when we visit them next week. Father won't see that hire-purchase is better than renting, will he?"

Jillian sighed. "Perhaps not," she said. "I wonder when we shall be able to afford a television."

It was at tea-time the following day that Jillian began talking again about television sets. "You know, your father was right last night. He said it would cost him much less to rent a set; at the end of one year he would have paid twice as much on hire-purchase. In fact, darling, I've been making enquiries at a television shop and the man said he would come and see us this evening."

Martin put his tea-cup down, surprised. "But I've been doing the same thing at another shop near the office," he said, "and my man will be coming round this evening, too."

A quarter of an hour later, Martin was in the living-room, listening to Jill's television agent and Jill was listening to Martin's man in the kitchen.

"Only £20 deposit," one man said, "and you will be watching television free for a year."

"Our television sets are so good," the other man said, "that after four years rent you will not have paid the cost of a set. And you'll have been saving your money."

Martin was just saying, "Yes, I'm sure we had better rent a set," when the telephone rang. It was his father, who said, "Martin, I've been thinking. You were right about renting a television set. It's better to buy one on hire-purchase." Martin was speechless. "So," his father went on, "we shall be getting a new set tomorrow. I'm ringing to ask if you would like our old one."

"Martin, darling," Jillian said later, "why did you suddenly get rid of the two television men?"

So Martin explained that they would be going round to his father's the following night to get their television set. "And we shan't be paying rent for it," he laughed.

Jillian sat down at the table with pencil and paper. "At the end of six months we'll have saved £12," she exclaimed. "Just think, we'll be watching television and we'll be saving money at the same time."

"There's only one thing," Martin said. "Next week is their silver wedding anniversary. We must get them a good present, especially when they've been so kind. How much do you suppose we ought to spend?"

"Twelve pounds?" asked Jillian in a small voice.

New words

hire-purchase, silver, an anniversary, golden, an occasion, a deposit, in advance, a set, to join in, an inquiry, the cost, to get rid of, especially.

Exercise 4

Read the story again before you answer these questions.

Why was Martin's father thinking of getting a new television set?
What did he want to ask Martin about?
How do you know Jillian was sitting near Martin?
Which did Martin think was better, hire-purchase or renting? How do you know?
Which did Martin's parents think was better? How do you know?
Why did both Martin and Jillian go and ask about television sets?
How many people were in Martin's flat when the telephone rang?
Why was Martin speechless when he heard what his father said?
How do you suppose Martin got rid of the two television men?
When Jillian sat down with pencil and paper, was she thinking about hire-purchase or renting?

Exercise 5

Two agents came to talk to Martin and Jillian. One was talking about hire-purchase, the other about renting. Here are some of the things they said. Write the sentences out in two lists, one for hire-purchase, the other for renting.

You will have paid for your set after two years.
You will never have paid for your set.
You will have paid £24 after one year.
You will have finished paying after two years.
You will have paid £47 in one year's time.
At the end of three years you'll have been spending less on your set.
You will have been buying your own set.
You won't have been buying your own set.
During the third year you'll have been paying nothing.
During the third year you'll have been paying £2 per month.

Exercise 6

Suppose you go to buy a camera on hire-purchase. The deposit is £40 the full cost is £100, and your payments are £5 at the end of each month. Like this:

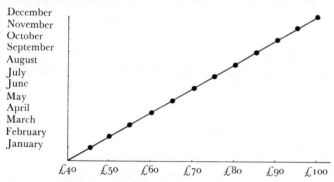

Practise with somebody.

Ask: How much shall I have paid at the end of — ?
Answer: You'll have paid — .
Ask: How long shall I have been buying it when I've paid £ — ?
Answer: You'll have been paying for — months.

Exercise 7

When Jillian thinks about "golden", these words come into her mind:

sun, ring, money, rich, daffodil.

Write down the English words that come into your mind when you think of the following:

an eye, midnight, an umbrella, wool, to lose, tobacco, to dance, December, soap, hard.

Exercise 8

Talk about yourself and people you know. Like this:

A   How long have you known John?
B   I met him the winter before last. I shall have known him two years next winter.

Then talk about things you have got. Like this:
A   How long have you had those shoes?
B   I bought them last June. I shall have had them a year next June.

And then talk about things you are doing. Like this:
A   How long have you been smoking a pipe?
B   I started in April two years ago. I shall have been smoking three years next April.

Exercise 9

Here are six sentences from the story. Without looking back, try to decide who spoke them, who they were talking to, and who they were talking about.

I knew you two would be coming.
I thought I would ask you what to do.
He said it would cost him less to rent a set.
He would have paid twice as much on hire-purchase.
He said he would come and see us this evening.
He explained that they would be going round to his father's the following night.

Then write down the words they said or thought in the first place. For example in the first sentence, Martin's father thought, "They will be coming."

Exercise 10   Conversation practice

Here are two short conversations between somebody making inquiries
by telephone about hiring cars, and somebody at the car-hire company.
In the first conversation, both people are speaking formally; in the second
much less formally. When you have practised the two conversations, try
putting an informal caller with a formal person in the office, and then
the other way round.

A   I understand you have cars for hire, and I would like to make inquiries
    about them.
B   Certainly. What is it you would like to know?
A   Have you a leaflet showing your prices?
B   Certainly. If you will let me have your name and address, I shall be
    delighted to post you full details.

A   Somebody said you've got cars you hire and I want to ask about them.
B   Right! What do you want to know?
A   Have you got a list that says what you have to pay?
B   Yes. Tell me your name and where you live and I'll send you all the
    details.

Unit 26

You can buy things, if you have some money
You can't buy things, unless you have some money

Exercise 1

Make sensible sentences about shopping in your own country.

| You | must
need to | have
save | — * if you | hope
want | to buy — .** |

* *(an amount of money)*   ** *(something in the shops)*

Now talk about the same things again, in another way.

| You can | buy
get | — ** if you have | got
saved | — .* |

And talk about the same things again, using "unless".

| You can't | buy
get | — ** | unless you have
if you haven't | got
saved | — .* |

He will come if you ask him

"You will hit your
head if you
aren't careful."

"You will hit your
head unless you
are careful."

Exercise 2

Look at these pictures

1   2

3

Several things might happen.

Picture 1
The man might stop walking.
He might start running.
He might hear or see the car coming.
The car might stop in time.
The car might hit the man.

Picture 2
The man might see the lion.
The girl might see the lion.
They might suddenly turn round.
The man might put his foot on the lion.
The lion might wake up and go away.

Picture 3
The pilot might see the car.
The man might jump out of the car.
The rope might break.
The plane might hit the bird.
The plane's engine might stop suddenly.

Say what you think will follow if these things happen. For example, in picture 1:

If the man stops walking, the car will hit him.

Exercise 3
Look at the three pictures again and make sensible sentences.

In the — * picture there'll be an accident unless — .**

* first	** he stops walking.	the lion moves.
second	he looks what he's doing.	they turn round.
third	the car stops.	he's very lucky.
	the plane stops.	he jumps out of the car.
	the rope breaks.	it's a dead lion.

He said he would come if you asked him

"I said you
would hit your
head if you
weren't careful."

26

Exercise 4

Look back at the pictures in Exercise 2 and remember what you said about them.

For example, I said that if the man stopped walking, the car would hit him.

A letter to the editor

Martin was alone in the flat waiting for Jillian to come home from an evening class. "She'll be feeling tired when she gets back," he thought. "She said last night she would watch that new television programme with me, if she got home in time. I've been looking forward to that all day."

Just then he caught sight of a woman's magazine lying open on the settee. He picked it up carelessly, but soon he was reading quite seriously. The magazine was open at the page of letters to the Editor, and the first letter went:

> *My husband and I have been married for six months now, but he has changed. He used to agree with me about everything, before we were married. But not now. If I say I like something, he says he hates it. If I want to stay in, he wants to go out. If I think we can't afford something, he thinks we can. In fact I know that if I ask him for something, he'll give me the opposite. So now, if I want to stay at home, I ask him to take me dancing.*
>
> *Are all men like this? We shall have been married six months next week, but already my romantic ideas are beginning to disappear.*
>
> *Yours unhappily,*
> *Young Wife*

Underneath, the Editor wrote that young people were often selfish; and that marriages would only be successful if husbands and wives tried to understand each other. But, possibly, six months after the wedding

251

was the most difficult time, because some people began to feel rebellious about then.

Martin put the magazine down. "We shall have been married six months soon." he thought. "If Jill reads this letter, she'll laugh. But perhaps she has read it. Perhaps she left the page open for me to see." He sat down, a worried expression on his face. If she thought he was getting rebellious, she would say so. And if she felt rebellious, she would tell him. "If she wants something, I usually agree," he said aloud.

And then he began to wonder. Perhaps he was too easy-going, too simple. Women were complicated and difficult to understand. Perhaps Jillian was telling him in a kind way that she was feeling rebellious. Perhaps she wanted him to be more complicated. "Well," he told himself, "if that's what she wants me to do, I will. It's true she likes arguing. Right. In future, if she says one thing, I'll say the opposite. So, if I want to go out, I shall have to say I want to stay in. In fact, unless I say I want to stay in, she won't want to go out."

He was starting to read the magazine letter again, when he heard Jillian coming in, and dropped it back onto the settee. "Hello, darling." Jillian said brightly. "If you want that television programme, you will have to be quick. It's time."

"That means she doesn't want to watch it," Martin thought. "Now if I want to see it, I must pretend I don't." So he said, "Oh I'm not very keen about it. In fact I'm tired. I think we ought to go to bed. You know, unless we start going to bed earlier, we shall get later and later every morning. Let's go to bed and read."

Jillian looked at him, surprised. "But we said if I got home early enough tonight we should watch the television together. Why did you ask me to do that if you wanted to go to bed early?" She looked at him, but he was speechless. "He'll get angry if I keep on talking about it," she thought. "Men are funny. I thought that programme was going to be interesting. Oh well, I am rather tired and there's that magazine I can read. So if he really wants to go to bed early, I'll agree."

"Come on, then. Get your book," she said.

Martin looked at the television set. "Of course, if you really want this programme, I'll stay up," he said. Jillian picked up her magazine from the settee and marched towards the bedroom calling, "Do as you like. I shall be reading in bed."

As Martin was putting his pyjamas on, Jillian started laughing at her magazine. "I say, darling," she said, "I've just read a letter here from a young woman who has been married six months. She said her husband never agreed with her. If she liked something, he hated it. If she wanted to stay in, he said he wanted to go out. If she thought they couldn't afford something, he said they could. So, do you know what she did? If she wanted to stay at home, she asked him to take her out. Isn't it silly?"

"Yes," Martin answered, sitting thinking on the side of the bed.

"And there's a lot of nonsense here about being selfish and feeling rebellious," Jillian said. "Why, we're not like that, are we? If you want to do something, I don't stop you. And if you think one thing, you don't tell me the opposite, do you? Here, where are you going, darling?"

He kissed her gently. "I'll be back in a minute," he said. "If you don't mind, I'll just go and see the end of that programme. You've got your magazine to read."

"Why," said Jillian, watching the bedroom door close, "why are men sometimes so complicated?"

New words

an editor, to catch sight of something, a magazine, a settee, to agree, opposite, selfish, a marriage, rebellious, aloud, easy-going, simple, complicated, to argue, brightly, to march, nonsense.

Exercise 5
Ask somebody:

What will you do if
    you find a spider in your bed tonight?
    the postman brings you a lot of money tomorrow?
    the next time you eat in a restaurant, you find you have no money?
    your boss tells you to find another job tomorrow?
    nobody remembers your next birthday?

What will happen if
    you get nothing to eat tomorrow?
    you don't go to work for a month?
    you lose this book?
    you can't find your shoes in the morning?
    your best friend starts to argue with you?

26

Exercise 6

Write these broken sentences together correctly.

A man will look for another job	if it hasn't any petrol.
A pen won't write	if they haven't got any pictures.
A musician will never be a good player	if it doesn't get any customers.
A car won't go	if he can't learn his words.
A doctor will never be successful	if she doesn't like books.
Children won't be interested in books	if there isn't any ink in it.
A tree won't live	if his boss doesn't pay him enough wages.
A shop will soon close	if he doesn't practise.
A librarian won't be happy	if he doesn't make his patients better.
A man will never be a good actor	if it can't get any water.

Exercise 7

Now write about the same things again, but this time using "unless".
Like this: A pen won't write unless there is some ink in it.

Exercise 8

Read the story again and answer these questions.

How did Martin think Jillian would be feeling when she got home?
What did "Young Wife" say her husband would give her if she asked for something?
Who said marriages would be successful if husbands and wives tried to understand each other?
What did Martin think Jillian would do if she read the letter?
What did Martin decide he would say if he wanted to go out?
What did he tell Jillian would happen unless they started going to bed earlier?
What did Jillian think Martin would do if she kept talking about the television programme?
What did Jillian say she would agree to do?

Why do you think Martin said he would stay up if Jillian really wanted the programme?

Why do you think Martin suddenly decided that, if Jillian didn't mind, he would go and watch the television?

Exercise 9

Write down the English words that come into your mind when you think of the following:

a blackboard, to run, a violin, whisky, to climb, green, an egg, to fly, a carpet, a bunch, noisy.

Exercise 10

Practise this part of a telephone conversation:

"Hello. Is that the Golden Ball Restaurant? Good. My name's Andrew Steel. I had lunch in the restaurant yesterday and I think I left my briefcase behind. It's light brown and it's got my name inside. Has anybody found it, please? No? Well, if you find it, would you mind ringing me? My number's 379 7281. Sorry to trouble you. Goodbye."

Now read this letter Mr Steel might have written to the restaurant manager, saying the same things.

> *22 The Drive,*
> *Newford.*
> *5th October, 1969.*
>
> *Dear Sir,*
> *I had lunch in your restaurant yesterday, but I think I left my briefcase behind. It is light brown and has my name inside. If anybody finds it, will you please telephone me at 379 7281 and I will come for it.*
>
> *I am sorry if I have troubled you.*
>
> *Yours faithfully,*
>
> *Andrew Steel*

Now pretend to telephone your local bus station or cinema, where you think you have left an umbrella or a parcel. Then write the letter making the same inquiry.

Unit 27

He would come if you asked him

Jillian can't switch the television on.
She can switch it on if she stands up.
She may, or she may not stand up.
She will be able to switch it on if she stands up.

She hasn't got a very, very long arm.
She could switch the television on if she had a very, very long arm.
That isn't possible.
She would be able to switch it on if she had a very, very long arm.

Exercise 1
Look at these five pictures.

1   2   3

27

4

5

Now write out correctly the five broken sentences.

If the man could run faster than the dog,	it would drink the water.
If the cat could fly,	it would stop walking.
If the horse could break the rope,	it would get out.
If the cow could open the door,	it would catch the bird.
If the elephant could read,	he would get away.

Now put these five sentences together correctly.

The dog wouldn't catch the man	if the cat could fly.
The bird wouldn't get away	if it could break the rope.
The horse wouldn't be thirsty	if it could read.
The cow wouldn't stay inside	if he could run faster than it.
The elephant wouldn't keep on walking	if it could open the door.

Exercise 2

Look at the five pictures in Exercise 1 again and imagine the animals can speak.
Now write five sentences like this: "If the — could speak, it would say —" (saying what you think they might say).
Then finish these sentences.

If the man bit the dog — .	If the door opened — .
If the bird fell dead — .	If the notice fell with a loud noise — .
If the rope broke — .	

Exercise 3

Practise with somebody.

Ask:	What	should	I we	be if	I we he she you they	worked	in a	restaurant? hospital? office? shop?
		would	he she you they				with a	car? camera?

Answer:	I We	should	be	a waiter. a nurse. a doctor.	waiters. nurses. doctors.
	He She You They	would		a secretary. a typist. a shop assistant. a driver. a photographer.	secretaries. typists. shop assistants. drivers. photographers.

If I were rich, I should be happy

"I wouldn't like to
    be in that car.
If I were in that car,
    I should be afraid.
But I would like to
    be younger.
If I were younger, I
    should like to
    drive a fast car."

27

Exercise 4

Let's pretend. What would you do if you were these things:

the richest person in the world
the cleverest person in the world
the biggest person in the world
the smallest person in the world
the most selfish person in the world

What would you do if you were these:
a lion, an elephant, a goldfish, a butterfly, a monkey?

Start every sentence: If I were — I should — .

Third time lucky

"Well, it's certainly nice to see you again, Tom," Martin said, giving him another drink. Tom laughed and looked across at Jillian.

"Yes," he answered. "The nurse said that if I went back into that hospital again, she would leave."

"You've been very unlucky," Jillian said, sympathetically.

"It's more than that," Tom said. "What would you think, if you went into hospital twice in six weeks? Would you just say it was unlucky if you broke your leg and then your arm immediately afterwards? If I were superstitious, I should be waiting for a third accident."

"Oh, don't let it get you down," Martin said. "It's all in the mind. If you want to stop thinking about accidents, you ought to go to a psychiatrist."

"Ha," said Tom. "If I walked into a psychiatrist's, I should fall over his carpet and break my wrist or something."

"Well," said Jill, joining in, "If you really are afraid of accidents, you'll have to go and have a quiet holiday in the country."

"But I've just had a quiet holiday in hospital," Tom shouted. "I want something new and exciting to do. Do you know, a friend rang up yesterday and asked if I would take his place in a motorcycle race. What would you say, Martin, if somebody asked you to do that?"

27

"Oh. I shouldn't want to do it," Martin answered. "What did you say?"

"I said no," Tom said sadly. "It would be exciting to ride in a race. But if I did, I'd have a crash. I'd hit somebody or somebody would hit me and I should wake up in an ambulance going to hospital."

They were silent for a moment, while Tom finished his drink. "Then," he said, "another friend asked me if I should like to start having flying lessons with him. What would you say to that, Martin, if you were me?"

"Flying must be great fun. I'd love to have lessons, if I could afford it," Martin said. "What did you say?"

"I asked if I could put it off for a few months. Well, if I went for lessons now, I should break something or the plane would have a crash."

"Oh, Tom, you're looking for trouble," Jillian said. "In any case, you wouldn't go up in a plane if you started now. You would have your first lessons on the ground. And you couldn't have a crash unless the plane was in the air, could you?"

"He might break his finger if he pressed the button to switch on," Martin laughed.

"You wouldn't think it was funny if you were me," Tom said. "But what would you two do if you thought you were going to have an accident? Would you take special care in everything you did? You know, if you are too careful, you often make yourself do things wrong."

"If I were absolutely sure I was going to have an accident," Martin said, "I think I should try to have a small one, deliberately."

"That's not so easy," Jillian said. "You only have accidents accidentally. No, I think if I were you I'd carry on as usual, and I shouldn't think about things going wrong."

"You're absolutely right, Jill," said Tom, jumping to his feet, and marching across the room to the door. "If I go home now, I shall have time to ring my friend about the flying lessons. Goodnight and thanks for a pleasant evening."

The front door closed and immediately afterwards there came a great crash, as if somebody had fallen downstairs. Jillian and Martin rushed breathlessly to the door. "I wonder if he's all right," Jill said.

At the bottom of the stairs sat Tom, blinking and feeling his legs and arms. They helped him to his feet.

"Thanks," he said, "I'm all right – nothing's broken. Oh, if I haven't broken anything, I can't call that my third accident, can I?"

"I think you can," Martin said and picked up Tom's glasses, broken into a hundred pieces.

Tom smiled. "Ah, good," he said. "I needed a new pair. I'll see better for my flying lessons."

New words

unlucky, sympathetically, immediately, afterwards, superstitious, to get somebody down, a psychiatrist, a race, a crash, to press, care, absolutely, to carry on, pleasant.

Exercise 5

Read the story again and answer these questions.

Why do you think the nurse would leave if Tom went back?

Would you think a third accident was coming if you broke your leg and then your arm?

Do you agree with Martin that a psychiatrist could help anybody who thought he was going to have an accident?

Do you agree with Tom that if he walked into a psychiatrist's, with accidents on his mind, he would break something?

Why wouldn't Martin ride in a motorcycle race if somebody asked him?

Why did Tom think he would have a crash if he rode in the race?

Martin would like to have flying lessons if he could; why does he think he can't?

Is Jillian right when she says that Tom wouldn't go up in a plane if it was only his first lesson?

Would you deliberately try to have a small accident, like Martin said, if you were superstitious and thought you would certainly have one?

If you were Jillian, would you tell Tom to carry on as usual?

27

Exercise 6

This man is on a desert island.

Imagine you are going to take his place.

If you knew you were going to live on a desert island, which animal would you take with you – a dog, a cat, a monkey, or a lion?

Which books, friends, records, clothes and equipment would you take with you? Say:

I	would wouldn't	take — because	it he she they	would wouldn't could couldn't might mightn't	— .

If I took —,	it he she they	would wouldn't could couldn't might mightn't	— .

262

27

Exercise 7

Answer these questions, using either "I shall" or "I should".

If you see a black cat tomorrow, what will you do?
If you saw a green cat tomorrow, what would you do?
If you don't sleep tonight, how will you feel?
If you didn't sleep for a week, how would you feel?
If somebody asks you to sing, what will you say?
If they asked you to sing on television, what would you say?
Which shop will you try if somebody asks you to buy some flour?
Which shop would you try if they asked you to buy an elephant?
What will you answer if somebody tells you he can't speak English?
What would you answer if he told you he couldn't speak?

Exercise 8

Look at these three pictures again.

1

2

3

Ask somebody:

Picture 1
What would you do if you were the man walking across the road?
What would you do if you were the driver?
What would you do if you saw this happening as you were passing?
What would you tell the police if you saw this accident happen?

Picture 2
What would you say if you were the girl?
What would you be saying if you were the man?
What would you do if you saw this happening when you were near?

Picture 3
What would you do if you were the man in the car?
What would you say to the pilot if you were a passenger in the plane?
What would happen to the man in the car if the plane took off?

Exercise 9
Look at each word on the left and find one word on the same line that
doesn't go with it.

to slide	to move	to go down	to run	to travel	to forget
to see	to hear	to watch	to empty	to listen	to look at
water	oil	wine	ink	fire	petrol
a colour	to dye	orange	paint	silent	to blush
to speak	to call	to say	to shout	to whisper	to sing

Exercise 10

Tom's friend asked if he would like to have flying lessons. When he telephoned Tom, he might have said:

FRIEND   I say, Tom, how would you like to learn to fly? You can have lessons with me at Blackfield Airport and they're not expensive. If you want to try, phone 01–636 5194 to book your first lesson. It's great fun.

But Tom might have seen an advertisement saying the same thing in a magazine or in the London underground. The advertisement might say:

> *Learn to fly!*
> *Inexpensive lessons at Blackfield Airport.*
> *Ring 01–636 5194 to book.*

Now tell Tom about dancing lessons and horse-riding lessons, and write advertisements for them.

Unit 28

He would have come if you had asked him

He didn't fall because the tree held him. He would have fallen if the tree hadn't held him.

The tree held him because his football shirt didn't tear. The tree wouldn't have held him if his football shirt had torn.

His football shirt didn't tear because he wasn't too heavy. His shirt would have torn if he had been too heavy.

He wasn't too heavy because he had played a lot of football. He would have been too heavy if he hadn't played a lot of football.

So – he would have fallen if he hadn't played a lot of football.
But – he wouldn't have fallen if he had not been playing football.

266

28

Exercise 1

Look at these three pictures again, and make twelve sentences about each.

1

2

3

In the first picture, the car didn't hit the man because he saw it coming, and also because the driver stopped.

The car	would might could	have hit the man	if he hadn't seen it coming. if the driver hadn't stopped. if he had kept on walking. if the driver had kept on going.

In the second picture, the lion didn't eat the two people, because they didn't touch it, and also because it didn't wake up.

The lion	would might could	have eaten them	if they had touched it. if it had woken up. if they hadn't seen it. if it hadn't kept on sleeping.

In the third picture, the plane didn't take the man into the air, because he jumped out of the car and also because the pilot didn't take off.

The plane	would might could	have taken the man up	if it had taken off. if he had stayed in the car. if the pilot hadn't stopped. if he hadn't jumped out.

Exercise 2

In these sentences, change the words underlined to make new, but true sentences.

If I had known it was so easy, I should have started English a long time ago.

If I had passed my examinations, I should have been a doctor by now.

If I had been luckier when I was seventeen, I should be in America now.

If it hadn't been so cold on Sunday, we shouldn't have gone to the cinema.

If we hadn't learnt at school, we should never have known how to do maths.

If Columbus had never discovered America, somebody else would have found it.

If my father had not met my mother, he would have married somebody else.

If my friend had seen the car coming, he would not have had his accident.

If you had never learned to read, you would not have started this book.

If all my relations had sent me birthday cards, they would have filled a shelf.

Exercise 3

Finish these sentences and write them.

If I had started saving money in the bank when I was fifteen, I might have — .

If I had started walking last Sunday, I could have got to — by now.

If I had eaten a big English breakfast this morning, I should — .

If — , I could have arrived earlier.

If — , I might never have met my best friend.

If — , he would have been the most important man in the world.

If you had posted a letter to me on Tuesday, it would have — .

If I had asked my father, he would have — .

If I had seen — , I might have — .

If you had gone to — for your holidays, you could have — .

The ice-cream van

"You would have gone straight into that ice-cream van, if I hadn't shouted," Martin said. "And if you had done, we might have had a bad crash." Jillian was practising driving Martin's car, and had stopped suddenly behind an ice-cream van.

"Nonsense," she said, gaily. "I want an ice-cream. And if I hadn't stopped here, you wouldn't have been able to buy me one."

As Martin got out of the car rather reluctantly, and joined the queue for ice-cream, Jillian switched on the car radio and, looking in the driving mirror, began to put more lipstick on.

Martin returned to the car a few minutes later, carrying two ice-creams and watching a huge, black dog that was following him. "If I were you, I'd eat this quickly," he said, giving Jillian her ice-cream. He got in, still looking fiercely at the dog. "I suppose if I'd been more careful, it wouldn't have happened, but that animal ate the first two ice-creams I bought. He just took them out of my hand."

"He wouldn't have got them if I had been buying them," Jillian thought. But at that moment the big dog jumped into the back of the car behind her. Martin laughed, as Jillian held her ice-cream away from it. "Oh, get out, you big horrible thing," she shouted. "Go away. Martin did you see that? He would have eaten mine too if I'd let him. Oh, get him out, Martin."

But, although Martin turned round in his seat and pushed, he couldn't move the dog. "Perhaps he'll go if you give him that last bit of your ice-cream," he said. But now people in the ice-cream queue were beginning to look and the music on the car radio suddenly stopped and a voice said, "Here is a police message. This afternoon the champion dog of Great Britain disappeared from its home in North London. If you have seen a large black dog, please tell your nearest police station. The police think that if thieves have taken the animal, it may still be in North London."

Immediately afterwards the dog started licking the back of Jillian's neck, Martin threw his arms round it to try to stop it and the ice-cream man started shouting at them from the van.

"Quick," Martin shouted. "Drive away. They think we're the thieves. If we stay here we shall never be able to explain, but if we stop again round the corner perhaps the dog will jump out."

Jillian reluctantly started the car. "If we *had* taken a champion dog," she called, "would we have stopped to buy ice-creams? But, perhaps this is the lost dog. And if it is, we had better take it to the police, hadn't we?"

Martin, half in the front seat and half in the back, shouted, "If you hadn't wanted an ice-cream, this wouldn't have happened." The car went round the corner on two wheels.

"Nonsense," Jillian shouted back. "If you hadn't given that dog two ice-creams, it would never have jumped into the car. And if it hadn't done that, nobody would have thought we were thieves."

Suddenly Jillian saw a policeman ahead of them and put the brakes on as hard as she could, so that the dog came flying out of the back seat and fell on top of Martin in the front. The car stopped beside the policeman as Martin's head appeared from under the dog.

"If I were you," the policeman said, "I should get a seat-belt for that animal."

28

"That," said Martin, "isn't very funny. But if you thought about doing your job, you would help us. We've found this dog, and we'd like to know if it's the champion dog that everybody's looking for?"

The policeman looked at the dog, then at Martin and Jillian. "You don't know much about dogs, do you?" he said. "That's no champion. Look at it. And if I wanted to know where it came from I should look for its address on its collar. Look, it comes from South London." Seeing them both speechless, he went on, "If I were you, I'd take it to the dogs' home. Unless you want to drive across London." And he walked away.

"I'm not driving for miles with this animal," Jillian said, fiercely, starting the car.

And two minutes later she stopped behind the ice-cream van once more. Immediately the huge black dog jumped out and ran to the head of the queue where a man was buying an ice-cream. It knocked the ice-cream out of his hand with its nose and ate it before anybody could speak. Jillian gasped. "If I hadn't seen that," she said, "I wouldn't have believed it. But I think I'd like another ice-cream darling, please."

When Martin got to the head of the queue again, the ice-cream man smiled. "I see you've brought my dog back. You needn't have done, you know. If you'd let him go, he would have come back by himself."

Now it was Martin's turn to gasp. "You mean it's your dog?" he said.

"Yes," the man laughed, "he follows me wherever I go and people seem to like to feed him. Funny isn't it?"

Martin paid for his two ice-creams and holding them high above his head, took them back to the car.

"If I had a gun," he began fiercely. . . . But Jillian was listening to the news reader on the car radio, who was saying that the police had found the champion dog.

New words

an ice-cream, a van, reluctantly, a mirror, to return, fiercely, a message, a champion, north, to lick, ahead, a brake, south, to gasp, to seem, to feed, a gun.

28

Exercise 4
Read the story again before answering these questions.

If you had been Martin, would you have gone reluctantly to buy Jillian's first ice-cream?

If you had been him, would you have let the dog get the first two? How would you have stopped it?

If you had been him, would you have laughed when the dog jumped into the back of the car? What would you have done?

If you had heard the police radio message and had seen the dog with Jillian and Martin, would you have thought they were thieves? What would you have done?

If you had been Jillian, would you have driven away with the dog in the back of the car? What would you have done?

If you had been her, would you have put your brakes on hard when you saw the policeman? What would you have done?

If you had been a policeman, would you have thought Jillian and Martin were thieves? What would you have thought?

If you had been Martin, would you have taken the dog back to the ice-cream van? What would you have done?

If you had been the ice-cream man, would you have told Martin he need not have brought the dog back? What would you have said?

If you had been the dog, how many ice-creams would you have eaten? How would you have felt?

Exercise 5
Practise your "if" sentences, by talking about countries and their languages.
If I go to — * I shall need to speak — .**

* England	Portugal	** English	Portuguese
France	Greece	French	Greek
Germany	Turkey	German	Turkish
Italy	Egypt	Italian	Arabic
Spain	Russia	Spanish	Russian

And now imagine living in those countries and say:
If I lived in — * I should speak — .**

And now suppose you had been born in those countries and say:
If I had been born in — * I should have learnt to speak — .**

Exercise 6

Think about the story again.

How do you know that Martin wasn't absolutely sure that Jillian wanted an ice-cream, at the beginning?

How do you know that he had to wait before he bought an ice-cream?

How did Jillian show that she knew she had to wait for her ice-cream?

How do you know what Jillian was listening to on the car radio?

When the ice-cream man started shouting at Jillian and Martin, what did they think he was saying? And what do you think he was saying?

How do you know what part of London this happened in?

How do you know which side of the road the policeman was walking on?

What makes you think that it was not an accident when the dog ate Martin's first two ice-creams?

Why did Martin hold the last ice-creams high above his head?

How do you think Martin was going to finish his last sentence, "If I had a gun . . ."?

Exercise 7

Practise with a friend, and ask:

If you had been born in	1800 1820 1850 1870 1900	how old would you	

have been in	1920? 1940? 1950? 1960?
be now?	

If you had been born in	England France Germany Italy Spain	which language would you

have learned first?
be speaking now?

Exercise 8

Look at these three pictures once again. Tell somebody to imagine the things are happening now.

1

2

3

28

Picture 1
What would you do if you were the car driver? If you were the man walking? If you were somebody passing by?

Picture 2
What would you do if you were the man? If you were the girl? If you were somebody passing by?

Picture 3
What would you do if you were the pilot? If you were the man in the car? If you were just passing by?

Now ask them to pretend that these things have happened, and ask them to imagine what they would have done. Ask three questions about each picture again, like this:
What would you have done if you had been the car driver?

Exercise 9
Here are four lists of words. Rewrite the lists, but putting the words in order of size, the greatest last.

huge, small, large, big.
whisper, shout, speak, call.

a lot, a couple, several, a few.
glad, pleased, delighted, happy.

Exercise 10
When a police message comes on the radio, it is usually rather more formal than if somebody was talking to a friend. Here is a police message:

An accident between a small green car and a bus took place at 1.45 p.m. yesterday afternoon on the corner of London Road and East Street, Sutton. Will anybody who may have seen the accident please telephone 241 7676, or their nearest police station.

28

And here is the same message in informal, more conversational language:

There was an accident between a little green car and a bus yesterday. It happened at a quarter to two on the corner of London Road and East Street, Sutton. If you saw it will you ring 241 7676, or your nearest police station.

Now write a police message and a more conversational one about an accident between a motorcycle (a motorbike) travelling west and a male pedestrian (a man walking), a short distance from (near) the Lion Hotel.

Unit 29

If he should hear, he would be angry

You may go to England.   If you went, you would hear a lot of English.
You might go to China.   If you should go, you would hear a lot of
Chinese.

Exercise 1
Finish these sentences, using the words given.

If a — bites a — , that isn't unusual. But if a — should bite a — , that
  would be unusual. (dog, man)
If you hear a bird — , it is not unusual. But if you should hear a bird — ,
  it would be unusual. (laughing, singing)
If a pretty girl wins a — , it is not unusual. But if she should win a — , it
  would be most unusual. (boxing match, beauty competition)
If you try to play — with a tennis ball, it's not impossible. But if you
  should try to play — with a football, it would be very difficult.
  (tennis, football)
If you ask an Englishwoman her — , it is polite. But if you should ask an
  Englishwoman her — , it is impolite. (age, name)

Exercise 2
Imagine what people might say or think about you. You don't think these
things will happen, but just in case, tell a friend:

		say tell you think		they would be wrong. they wouldn't be right.
If	anyone should		that I'm — *	
	you should hear			it wouldn't be true. it would be untrue.

* stupid, very rich, dangerous, lazy, unfriendly, miserable, fierce, selfish
  rebellious, impatient.

29

If you will come, we can play

MARTIN If you will lend me a
pound, I can pay.

JILLIAN I've only got one pound.
But you may have it, if you'll pay me
back when we get home.

MARTIN Certainly. I've left my
money in my other suit.

Exercise 3

Finish these sentences using the words given.

If you will help me with my homework, father, my teacher might be
   pleased with me — . Certainly I'll help you, if you'll go to bed early — .
   (tonight, tomorrow)

If you will — me the money I can go to England for my holidays. I might
   lend you it, if you will let me — your car while you're away. (borrow,
   lend)

If you'll write regularly, I'll give you the — of an English pen-friend. Of
   course I will, and if she'll let me go and stay with her, she can have a
   holiday at my — . (address, home)

I'll open the new — if you'll have another — of wine. No thanks, I'm
   driving home; but I'll drink to you when I get there if you'll give me
   the — to take with me. (glass, bottle)

If you'll help me push the car it might go. Certainly. If you'll let me take
   the wheel, I'll — while you — . (drive, push)

29

The picnic

It was a Sunday morning and Jillian was getting ready to go out for a picnic. Martin was not very keen to go and started making difficulties.

"It may rain," he said. "Or we may not be able to find a field to eat in. Or perhaps the car will break down. . . ."

"Oh, really!" Jillian exclaimed fiercely, dropping a packet of butter into the picnic basket. "You're looking for difficulties. If it should rain," she went on, putting a carton of milk with the butter, "we can eat in the car, with the roof on. And if all the good picnic places should be full," and she put a plastic box of sugar into the basket, "we'll drive on until we find somewhere. And even if the car should break down, we'll eat our picnic wherever it stops." She put the flask of coffee on top of the food and waited for Martin's next objection. But he was looking at the newspaper. Suddenly he said, "Listen to this, Jill," and read out:

"Mr Gordon Lister, of Luton, who took his family into a field for a picnic, one day last week, had just unpacked the food from the car when Mrs Lister saw a notice a little distance away. 'Don't go and read it,' Mr Lister told his family. 'If it should say "Private" we'll have to go.' Later, having finished eating, they walked over to the notice, which said 'Beware of snakes'."

Jillian laughed. "I don't think I would have stayed in that field very long, if I'd been there," she said.

"Yes," Martin answered, "and what will you do if there should be snakes in this place we're going to?"

"I've got a big strong man to look after me in case I should need it," Jillian answered sweetly. "Come on."

Two hours later, Martin parked the car at the side of a quiet river where there was an open field and a notice saying "Picnic Place". He got out reluctantly and watched Jillian choosing a good place to sit. "Come on, Martin," she called. "It's super. And bring the picnic basket, in case we should feel hungry."

"I wouldn't sit here, if I were you," he said, joining her. "Think of the snakes."

"Oh shut up," she answered, "and look at what's in the basket."

"I have done," he said, smiling and holding up a can of beer. "If I'd known this was in here I would have driven here faster. I say, where's the can opener? If we should have come without it. . . ." But Jillian was already passing it to him. "You know," he went on, "it's a pity that notice is there. If other people should see it, they'll be stopping here too and we shall have a crowd."

"Then go and cover it," Jillian said, starting to unpack the basket, and passing Martin a large sheet of paper. "You go and do that, if it will make you happy, while I get the picnic ready."

Martin came back looking very pleased with himself. "There," he said, "if anyone should see the notice now, they won't know this is a picnic place. Come on, I'm hungry. Open the basket."

"I have done," Jillian said, passing him a piece of cold chicken. "Help yourself."

They were still sitting on the grass and eating when a car stopped a short distance from the notice. The driver and his passengers had a short conversation, but decided to go somewhere else. But before he drove away, the man called across to Jillian and Martin, "Keep your eyes open for snakes." And he laughed.

"Mm," Jillian said, "he's been reading the newspaper. I'm glad they didn't decide to stay. If they had done, I don't think we would have been here long. It would have become too noisy."

Then suddenly she jumped to her feet. "Martin, there's a snake," she called.

"Oh nonsense," he said casually. "I wouldn't bring you to a picnic place if it was full of snakes." Then he jumped up. "Good heavens, you're right. Come on, let's pack this basket and go."

As quickly as they could, they collected their picnic things. "If you take the basket to the car," Jillian said, "I'll go and take your sheet of paper off the notice."

She joined Martin in the car a moment later, but without the sheet of paper. "I've left it there," she said, "in case anyone else should think this is a good picnic place."

Slowly they drove past the picnic notice. Martin's paper still covered it, and they both read the words he had written on it – "Beware of snakes".

"I thought it was a good idea," he said sadly. "But obviously snakes can read."

New words

a picnic, a difficulty, a field, to break down, a packet, a carton, a flask, an objection, to unpack, private, to beware of, a snake, a river, to choose, a can, a can opener, to cover, a sheet, a chicken, to become, casually, good heavens, to collect, obviously.

29

Exercise 4

Read the story again and write answers to these questions. Practise saying your answers first, using "I'd", but when you write them, use "I should".

If you had been Martin, would you have been keen to go for a picnic?

If you had been Jillian, would you have chosen to take the same food, or some other?

If you had been Mr Lister, would you have told your family not to read the notice?

If you have been Martin, would you have stopped at the picnic place?

If you had been Martin, would you have been glad to find the can of beer?

If you had been Jillian, what would you have thought Martin was doing with the sheet of paper?

If you had been Martin, would you have written a new notice on the paper?

If you had been in the car that arrived, would you have wanted to stay or go away?

If you had been Jillian, would you have thought the other people had read the same newspaper?

If you had been Martin, would you have thought the same thing?

If you had been Jillian, would you have left Martin's notice covering the old one?

If you had been her, what would you have answered to Martin when he said, "Obviously snakes can read"?

Notice how you start to say a "Yes" answer with "I'd have — ", but a "No" answer starts "I shouldn't have — ".

Exercise 5

Now write answers to these questions. Practise saying your answers, using "I'd", but when you write them, use "I would".

Would you go for a picnic with Jillian, if she asked you?

Would you go out in Martin's car, if he asked you?

Would you eat a picnic in the car, if it rained?

Would you have a picnic near a notice that said "Beware of snakes"?

Would you go into a field with a notice that said "Private"?

Would you stay in a picnic place if a crowd of other people came?
Would you sit on the grass to eat, if there was no danger of snakes?
Would you stay to collect your picnic things, if you saw a snake?
Would you try to kill a snake, if you saw one?
Would you always carry a basket for your wife, even if it was light?

Notice how you start to say a "Yes" answer with "I'd", but a "No" answer with "I wouldn't".

Exercise 6
Imagine a friend is going shopping and might see something you've been looking for. Ask them to buy it for you.

If you should	see notice find	a — * of — **	would you buy would you mind buying

one for me.
me one.

* packet, carton, box, tin, can, bottle, tube.

** china tea, green paint, chocolate ice-cream, typing paper, milk, envelopes, orange juice, toothpaste, eggs, glue, face powder, shampoo.

Notice how your friend agrees – "Yes, I will" or "No, I don't mind."

Exercise 7
Let's pretend. Ask somebody:

If somebody should ask you to appear on television, which programme would you choose?
If somebody should say they would buy you an English car, which kind would you choose?
If somebody should tell you you had to live in another country, which one would you decide on?

If somebody should say you had to change your name, what new name would you choose?

If somebody should say you could become any famous person in history, who would you be?

Suppose you were in a plane. If the pilot should say there was going to be a crash, what would you do?

Suppose you were in a boat. If it should start to go down, what would you do?

If your doctor should say you are going to die next week, what would you do?

If you should arrive home to find your house on fire, what would you do?

If you should be able to change things into gold by touching them, what would you touch first?

Exercise 8

Put these broken sentences together correctly.

It didn't rain, but if it had done	they would have eaten where it stopped.
The car didn't break down, but if it had done	he wouldn't have had the picnic near the notice.
Mr Lister didn't read the notice, but if he had done	he wouldn't have said, "Oh nonsense."
Martin didn't pack the basket, but if he had done	he would have driven to the picnic more quickly.
He didn't know there was some beer, but if he had done	they could not have opened the beer can.
Jillian didn't forget the can-opener, and if she had done	the picnic place might have become too noisy.
She didn't see Martin write his new notice, and if she had done	they would have eaten in the car.
The people in the other car didn't stay, but if they had done	other people might have used the picnic place.
Martin didn't see the snake first, but if he had done	he would have known there was some beer in it.
Jillian didn't take the paper off the notice, and if she had done	she might have thought he was silly.

29

Exercise 9

Here is a list of words. Think about them carefully, and then decide which ones are usually round and which are square. Then decide which ones are usually hard and which are soft.

an apple, a pencil, a can, a carton, a box, an orange, a ball of wool, a wheel, a shilling, a book.

Which ones would break if you dropped them? Which ones would not change if they fell from an aeroplane?

Exercise 10

Read the story again that Martin read from the newspaper about the Lister family. That was written in rather formal English. But if somebody told the story, informally, to a friend, he might put it like this:

There was a man called Gordon Lister. He lived in Luton, and one day last week he took his family into a field for a picnic. They'd just unpacked the food when Mrs Lister saw a notice a little way off. Mr Lister said, "Don't go and read it. It might say 'Private' and then we'll have to go." Later, when they'd finished eating, they walked over to the notice. It said, "Beware of Snakes".

Now read this little story from a newspaper and tell it again, but in informal language, to a friend.

Mr Alan Black, whose house is very close to a large football ground, often has difficulty on Saturday afternoons, because people park their cars outside the entrance to his garage. Arriving home last Saturday to find that he could not use his own garage because of a large car in the entrance, he grew so angry that he let the air out of all four tyres. His wife met him a moment later as he entered the house, with the news that the new vicar was waiting to see him and had left his car in their entrance.

Unit 30

I wish he would come

I wish the rain would stop.
I wish I was in a car.
I wish I didn't hate getting wet.

Exercise 1
Tell the truth about the things in this list, saying either:
I wish I could — . *or* I've never wished I could — .
be beautiful, be rich, be taller, be a champion tennis player, be a pop
singer, fly, swim, play the violin, live in America, read faster.

Do the same with this list, using either:
I wish I didn't — . *or* I've never wished I didn't — .
blush, dance, drink, like food, learn English, smoke, need to sleep, laugh
so loudly, have to work, worry so much.

I wish he had come

I wish the rain had stopped earlier.
I wish I hadn't come out.
I wish I had brought a boat with me.

30

Exercise 2

Look at the six photographs of Martin again, and then read the list of sentences. Decide which picture each sentence goes with.

1
*My first long
trousers. Age 12.*

2
*At the swimming
pool. Age 8.*

3
*After my first driving
lesson. Age 17.*

4
*An early walk
with Jill. Age 20.*

5
*My first car.
Age 21.*

6
*In the mountains.
Age 21.*

I wish I had noticed that tree.
I wish I hadn't taken the dog.
I wish I had caught a fish.
I wish I had cleaned the car more carefully.
I wish I had tried not to cry.

I wish I had asked her to stand closer.
I wish I had bought a few more flowers.
I wish I had taken my hands out of my pockets.
I wish I had chosen a different instructor.
I wish I had stopped smoking for a minute.
I wish I had asked her to look at the camera.
I wish I hadn't hated the lessons.

Exercise 3

Instead of "I wish", we can say "If only". For example, in the two pictures of Jillian on her scooter at the beginning of this Unit, she might think: "If only the rain would stop" and "If only the rain had stopped".

Now do Exercise 2 again, but saying "If only" instead of "I wish".

You should be careful

You shouldn't drive in the rain.
You should have stayed at home.
should = ought to

Exercise 4

Say three things that people should do and three things they shouldn't do:

in a library, in church, in a classroom, at a party, in a small boat.
when they are swimming, when they are driving, when they are eating.

Then ask someone to say when you should and when you shouldn't:
wear a hat, sing, run, wear boots, ask how much something costs.

30

The birthday present

"Peter tells me it's Martin's birthday tomorrow," Liz said at the other end of the telephone. Jillian gasped.

"Good heavens, if you hadn't said that, I should have forgotten," she said, blushing, although there was no one in the room to see her. "If only I could think of something to buy him!" she sighed. "Can you think of anything, Liz? I wish I could."

There was a moment's pause, before Liz said, "How about buying him a new tennis racket? I think Peter and Martin have been playing together lately. He should like that."

"Yes, he should," Jillian answered, thinking, "He certainly would, if I could afford it. Thanks for the suggestion, Liz," she said. "If I'm going to go out shopping, I'd better stop talking. If I should forget Martin's birthday present, he wouldn't be very pleased. Bye bye."

"I would have bought a racket if I could have afforded it," Jillian thought, coming back into the flat from the sports shop, with a box of new tennis balls. "He'll like these. But I wish he'd told me he was starting to play tennis again." She was looking enviously at the new balls when the telephone rang. It was Liz once more.

"I say, Jill," she said, "I wish I hadn't told you about our two men playing tennis together. Because I was wrong. I've just discovered they've been playing squash. You haven't bought a racket already, have you?" Jill looked hard at the telephone.

"No," she answered. "Thanks for ringing. But if you should hear they've been playing ice hockey, or something, please let me know. Bye-bye."

"If only I had waited for a few minutes before I went to the shop!" she thought. "Anyway it's my fault. I shouldn't have gone rushing off when Liz had an idea. I wonder if the shop will change these for squash balls?"

"I wonder if you would mind changing these tennis balls for squash balls?" Jillian asked the assistant sweetly. "I'm afraid I've made a mistake. I should be more careful, I know."

The man came back with a smaller box with six squash balls in it. "If these should be wrong," he said, with a smile, "just let us know."

But when she arrived home again, Martin had got there before her. She could hear him changing in the bedroom, but before she called to him her eye fell on the settee, where he had thrown his briefcase. Lying on top of it was a racket, not a squash racket but a badminton racket. "Liz has made a mistake," she thought. "It's badminton they've been playing. Oh, if only I hadn't changed the tennis balls for these squash balls! Oh dear, I should have made my own mind up in the first place." She went out of the flat door as quietly as possible, thinking, "I wonder if the shop will change these for badminton shuttles?"

"I wonder if you would mind changing these squash balls for shuttle-cocks?" Jillian asked the assistant very sweetly. "I'm afraid I've made another mistake. I really must be more careful, I know."

The man came back with a large tube of shuttlecocks. "If these should be wrong," he said with an icy smile, "I may not be able to change them."

Jillian rushed out of the shop with the shuttlecocks, thinking fiercely, "I wish I had bought him a pair of socks, or something uninteresting." As she entered the living-room she put Martin's present behind her back. He looked up, as she came in, the badminton racket in his hand. "Hello darling. This is Tom's. He asked me if I'd take it in for a new string, because I said I might be going to the sports shop. Oh, I didn't tell you, did I? Father sent me some money for my birthday so I've ordered a new tennis racket from the sports shop. I thought it was time I started playing again. I had a game of squash with Peter last week, but I'd rather play tennis with you."

Jillian turned to the mirror on the wall, thinking, "If only I didn't blush so easily." Then she said, "Martin, I'm going round to the sports shop myself in a minute. Would you like me to collect your new racket?"

"I wish you would," he said. "Oh, and if anyone should ask you what I'd like for my birthday, you can always suggest some new tennis balls."

"You shouldn't tell people what presents to buy you," she laughed, picking up Tom's racket and hiding the tube of shuttlecocks as she went out. "They may have bought something already."

The same assistant met Jillian in the sports shop. She put the badminton racket and shuttlecocks on the counter, looked him straight in the eyes and said, "Now it's a long story and you must be patient. . . ."

New words

no one, a pause, a racket, a suggestion, bye-bye, enviously, squash, hockey, anyway, badminton, to make one's mind up, a shuttlecock, icy, to enter, a string, to order, to suggest.

Exercise 5
Read the story again, before answering these questions:

Which words tell you that Jillian was surprised during her first conversation with Liz?
How do you know she felt guilty?
Why did Jillian stop her telephone conversation?
How do you know Jillian likes playing tennis?
Why did Liz ring to ask if Jillian had bought a new tennis racket?
Which words show that Jillian was trying to be polite when she took the tennis balls back?
How do you know that the assistant was becoming less pleased when she took the squash balls back?
Why did Jillian wish she had bought Martin a pair of socks?
Why did Jillian turn to the mirror after Martin had spoken to her?
What was Jillian going to tell the assistant at the end of the story?

Exercise 6
Notice how Liz said, "How about buying him a new tennis racket?" This is an informal suggestion. When Jillian said, "I wonder if you would mind . . ." she was being more formal.

Practise these conversations, giving formal answers to formal invitations, and informal ones to informal invitations.

A { How about having lunch with me?
{ I wonder if you would like to join me for lunch?
B { Fine. Thanks very much.
{ I should be delighted. Thank you.
A { How about the Green Man on Monday, at, say, one fifteen?
{ Could you meet me at the Green Man Hotel on Monday, at a quarter past one?
B { It's a date. Bye for now.
{ Certainly, I shall be there. Goodbye until then.

Practise again, changing the time and place. Instead of lunch, you might ask someone to dinner (in the evening), or a drink (in a pub).

30

Exercise 7

Imagine an Englishman is coming to stay in your own country for the first time and he asks you to tell him the things he should know and do: Starting each sentence with either "You should" or "You shouldn't", tell him three things about each of the following:

hiring a car, driving in your country, sending a letter to England, staying in a hotel, eating local food, places to visit.

When you have told him, ask about the same things in England. Use "should" in each case.

Exercise 8

Practise with a friend.

I wish If only	you would	wash your — .* clean your — .** give me — .***

    * car, windows, hair, hands.
  ** shoes, room, teeth, nails.
*** a drink, some food, some money.

But I have done. I	washed cleaned	it them	— .****
	gave you	one some	

**** this morning, on Monday (etc.), last week, last month, last year.

30

Exercise 9
Here are twelve English verbs:

to argue, to blink, to cry, to gasp, to hate, to jump, to laugh, to look forward to something, to lose something, to shout, to sigh, to smile.

Find three which you do when you are angry, three that you do when you are surprised, three you do when you are happy, and three when you are sad. Then think about them again, and decide which verbs use (a) your eyes, (b) your mouth, and (c) your mind only.

Exercise 10
Jillian took her present of tennis balls back to the sports shop when she wanted to change them for squash balls. If she had sent them back, she might have written the following letter.

15 Bridge St,
Hampstead
16 May 1970

Dear Sirs,
    I am returning these tennis balls which I bought in your shop yesterday, hoping that you will kindly change them for squash balls. I'm afraid I made a mistake when I bought them.

    Would you mind sending the squash balls to the above address and let me know if there is anything further to pay?

      Yours faithfully,

      Jillian Fry (Mrs)

Now write the letter that she might have written when she wanted to change the squash balls.

Then try to make up the telephone conversation between Jillian and the shop assistant if she had rung the shop up to ask if they would mind changing the tennis balls for squash balls.

Word list

This list shows all the words of *Coursebooks* 1 and 2, except numbers. The figures after each word refer to the Coursebook and Unit in which the word first appears.

an attendant [ə'tendənt] 2, **23**
an attic ['ætik] 2, **9**
   August ['ɔ:gəst] 1, **31**
an aunt [ɑ:nt] 1, **12**
   Austria ['ɔ:striə] 1, **32**
an autumn ['ɔ:təm] 2, **6**
   away [ə'wei] 1, **12**
   away from [ə'wei frəm] 1, **9**
   awful ['ɔ:fl] 1, **30**
   awfully ['ɔ:fli] 2, **22**

a baby ['beibi] (babies) 2, **2**
   back [bæk] 1, **17**
a back [bæk] 1, **33**
   bad [bæd] (worse, worst) 1, **3**
   badly ['bædli] 1, **28**
   badminton ['bædmintən] 2, **30**
a bag [bæg] 1, **7**
   bah [bɑ:] 2, **2**
   Baker St ['beikə stri:t] 2, **24**
a ball [bɔ:l] 1, **16**
a ballpen ['bɔ:lpen] 2, **12**
a ballpoint ['bɔ:lpɔint] 2, **24**
a banana [bə'nɑ:nə] 2, **14**
a bank [bæŋk] 2, **21**
a bar [bɑ:] 2, **13**
a barman ['bɑ:mən] (barmen) 2, **20**
a basin ['beisn] 1, **24**
a basket ['bɑ:skit] 2, **20**
a bat [bæt] 1, **16**
a bath [bɑ:θ] 1, **4**
a bathroom ['bɑ:θrum] 1, **4**
the B.B.C. [bi: bi: si:] 1, **32**
to be [bi:]
      am [æm] 1, **3**
      are [ɑ:] 1, **2**
      been [bi:n, bin] 1, **24**
      is [iz] 1, **1**
      was [wɔz, wəz] 1, **26**
      were [wə:, wə] 1, **26**
to be able [bi: 'eibl] 2, **17**
to be born [bi: bɔ:n] 2, **28**
a beard [biəd] 2, **23**
to beat [bi:t] (beat, beaten) 1, **24**
a beater ['bi:tə] 1, **24**

beautiful ['bju:tifəl] 1, **22**
   beauty ['bju:ti] 2, **29**
   because [bi'kɔz] 1, **19**
to become [bi'kʌm] (became, become) 2, **29**
a bed [bed] 1, **4**
a bedroom ['bedrum] 1, **4**
a bedtime ['bedtaim] 1, **17**
   beer [biə] 1, **21**
   before[1] [bi'fɔ:] 1, **24**
   before[2] [bi'fɔ:] 1, **25**
to begin [bi'gin] (began, begun) 2, **1**
a beginner [bi'ginə] 2, **20**
the beginning [bi'giniŋ] 1, **33**
   behind [bi'haind] 1, **16**
   Belgium ['beldʒəm] 2, **25**
to believe [bi'li:v] (believed) 2, **28**
a bell [bel] 1, **20**
a belt [belt] 2, **20**
   below [bi'lou] 2, **19**
   Ben [ben] 1, **23**
   Benny ['beni] 2, **6**
   Berlin [bə'lin] 1, **35**
   beside [bi'said] 2, **18**
   best [best] (see good, well)
   better ['betə] (see good, well)
   between [bi'twi:n] 2, **4**
to beware [bi'wɛə] 2, **29**
a bicycle ['baisikl] 1, **20**
   big [big] (bigger, biggest) 1, **5**
a bill [bil] 1, **34**
   Bill [bil] 1, **3**
   binoculars [bi'nɔkjuləz] 1, **19**
a bird [bə:d] 1, **1**
a birthday ['bə:θdei] 1, **33**
a bit [bit] 2, **1**
to bite [bait] (bit, bitten) 2, **24**
   black [blæk] 1, **4**
a blackboard ['blækbɔ:d] 2, **3**
to blink [bliŋk] (blinked) 2, **23**
   blood [blʌd] 1, **14**
a blouse [blauz] 1, **3**
   blue [blu:] 1, **8**
to blush [blʌʃ] (blushed) 2, **23**
a boat [bout] 2, **29**
a bob [bɔb] 2, **23**

a body ['bɔdi] (bodies) 2, **1**
Bonzo ['bɔnzou] 1, **10**
a book [buk] 1, **10**
to book [buk] (booked) 1, **36**
a bookshelf ['bukʃelf] (-shelves) 1, **23**
a boot¹ [buːt] 1, **18**
a boot² [buːt] 1, **25**
a bootlace ['buːtleis] 1, **20**
to borrow ['bɔrou] (borrowed) 1, **34**
a borrower ['bɔrouə] 2, **11**
a boss [bɔs] 1, **32**
both [bouθ] 1, **33**
a bottle ['bɔtl] 1, **6**
a bottom ['bɔtəm] 1, **31**
Bournemouth ['bɔːnməθ] 2, **7**
a bowl [boul] 1, **26**
bowling ['bouliŋ] 1, **16**
a box [bɔks] (boxes) 1, **5**
to box [bɔks] (boxed) 1, **18**
a boxer ['bɔksə] 1, **18**
a boy [bɔi] 1, **3**
a brake [breik] 2, **28**
brass [brɑːs] 2, **6**
Brass [brɑːs] 2, **3**
bread [bred] 1, **21**
to break [breik] (broke, broken) 1, **20**
to break down [breik daun] (broke, broken) 2, **29**
a breakfast ['brekfəst] 1, **16**
breathless ['breθləs] 2, **24**
breathlessly ['breθləsli] 2, **24**
a bride [braid] 2, **18**
a bridge [bridʒ] 1, **23**
a briefcase ['briːfkeis] 2, **5**
bright [brait] 2, **23**
brightly ['braitli] 2, **26**
to bring [briŋ] (brought, brought) 1, **18**
to bring back [briŋ bæk] (brought, brought) 2, **9**
to bring down [briŋ daun] (brought, brought) 2, **9**
to bring in [briŋ in] (brought, brought) 2, **9**
to bring round [briŋ raund] (brought, brought) 2, **11**
broad [brɔːd] 1, **18**

broken ['broukn] 1, **20**
a brother ['brʌðə] 1, **8**
brown [braun] 1, **8**
a brush [brʌʃ] (brushes) 1, **34**
Brussels ['brʌslz] 1, **35**
a building ['bildiŋ] 2, **23**
a bunch [bʌnʃ] (bunches) 2, **16**
to burst into [bəːst'intu] (burst, burst) 2, **15**
to burst out [bəːst aut] (burst, burst) 2, **13**
a bus [bʌs] (buses) 1, **8**
but¹ [bʌt] 1, **1**
but² [bʌt] 2, **6**
butter ['bʌtə] 1, **21**
a butterfly ['bʌtəflai] (butterflies) 1, **11**
a button ['bʌtn] 1, **10**
to buy [bai] (bought, bought) 1, **17**
by¹ [bai] 1, **33**
by² [bai] 2, **9**
bye-bye [bai bai] 2, **30**

a cake [keik] 1, **24**
a calendar ['kælində] 1, **32**
to call¹ [kɔːl] (called) 2, **2**
to call² [kɔːl] (called) 2, **8**
a caller ['kɔːlə] 2, **22**
a camera ['kæmərə] 1, **11**
can [kæn] 1, **25**
a can [kæn] 2, **29**
to cancel ['kænsəl] (cancelled) 1, **36**
a captain ['kæptən] 2, **22**
a car [kɑː] 1, **2**
a card [kɑːd] 2, **2**
care [kɛə] 2, **27**
careful ['kɛəfl] 1, **11**
carefully ['kɛəfli] 1, **28**
careless ['kɛələs] 2, **12**
carelessly ['kɛələsli] 2, **7**
a carpet ['kɑːpit] 1, **4**
to carry ['kæri] (carried) 1, **33**
a carton ['kɑːtən] 2, **29**
a cartoon [kɑː'tuːn] 2, **22**
a case [keis] 1, **19**
in case [in keis] 2, **29**

in any case [in eni keis] 2, **20**
  a cashier [kæˈʃiə] 1, **25**
    casually [ˈkæʒjuəli] 2, **29**
  a cat [kæt] 1, **34**
  a catalogue [ˈkætələg] 2, **23**
  to catch [kætʃ] (caught, caught) 2, **16**
  to catch sight of [kætʃ sait əv]
    (caught, caught) 2, **26**
  a centre [ˈsentə] 2, **20**
    certainly [ˈsəːtənli] 2, **3**
  a chair [tʃɛə] 1, **2**
  a champion [ˈtʃæmpiən] 2, **28**
  to change [tʃeindʒ] (changed) 2, **6**
  a changing room [ˈtʃeindʒiŋ rum] 2, **8**
  a chap [tʃæp] 2, **20**
    cheap [tʃiːp] 1, **6**
    cheaply [ˈtʃiːpli] 2, **7**
  a cheek [tʃiːk] 2, **19**
    cheese [tʃiːz] 1, **21**
    chicken [ˈtʃikin] 2, **29**
  a child [tʃaild] (children) 1, **12**
  a chin [tʃin] 1, **26**
    China [ˈtʃainə] 2, **29**
    chocolate [ˈtʃɔklət] 2, **29**
  to choose [tʃuːz] (chose, chosen) 2, **23**
    Christina [krisˈtiːnə] 2, **6**
  a church [tʃəːtʃ] (churches) 2, **17**
  a cigarette [sigəˈret] 2, **3**
  a cinema [ˈsinimə] 1, **15**
  a class [klɑːs] 2, **14**
  a classroom [ˈklɑːsrum] 2, **30**
    clean [kliːn] 1, **33**
  to clean [kliːn] (cleaned) 1, **34**
  to clean up [kliːn ʌp] (cleaned) 1, **34**
  a cleaner [ˈkliːnə] 1, **9**
  a clergyman [ˈkləːdʒimən]
    (clergymen) 2, **3**
    clever [ˈklevə] 1, **3**
  to climb [klaim] (climbed) 1, **18**
  a climber [ˈklaimə] 1, **18**
  a clock [klɔk] 1, **16**
  to close [klouz] (closed) 2, **20**
    close [klous] 2, **18**
    closely [ˈklousli] 2, **14**
    clothes [klouðz] 1, **3**
  a cloud [klaud] 2, **19**

    cloudy [ˈklaudi] 1, **35**
  a club [klʌb] 2, **20**
  a coat [kout] 1, **34**
    coffee [ˈkɔfi] 1, **10**
    cold [kould] 1, **7**
    coldly [ˈkouldli] 2, **22**
  a collar [ˈkɔlə] 1, **23**
  a college [ˈkɔlidʒ] 1, **32**
  a colour [ˈkʌlə] 1, **23**
  to collect [kəˈlekt] 2, **29**
    Columbus [kəˈlʌmbəs] 2, **28**
  to come [kʌm] (came, come) 1, **9**
  to come back [kʌm bæk] (came,
    come) 2, **2**
  to come home [kʌm houm] (came,
    come) 2, **9**
  to come in [kʌm in] (came, come) **2**, **2**
  to come on[1] [kʌm ɔn] (came,
    come) 1, **22**
  to come on[2] [kʌm ɔn] (came,
    come) 2, **10**
  to come out [kʌm aut] (came,
    come) 2, **9**
  to come round [kʌm raund] (came,
    come) 2, **9**
  to come up [kʌm ʌp] (came,
    come) 2, **24**
    comfortable [ˈkʌmfətəbl] 1, **14**
    comfortably [ˈkʌmfətəbli] 1, **29**
  a company [ˈkʌmpəni] 1, **29**
  a competition [kɔmpəˈtiʃn] 2, **10**
    complicated [ˈkɔmplikeitid] 2, **26**
  a concert [ˈkɔnsət] 2, **14**
    congratulations [kənˈgrætjuˈleiʃnz]
    2, **2**
    conversation [kɔnvəˈseiʃn] 2, **1**
    conversational [kɔnvəˈseiʃənəl] 2, **28**
  a cook [kuk] 2, **22**
  to cook [kuk] (cooked) 2, **22**
    cookery [ˈkukəri] 2, **22**
    cool [kuːl] 1, **35**
    coolly [ˈkuːlli] 2, **24**
  to copy [ˈkɔpi] (copied) 2, **17**
  a corner [ˈkɔːnə] 2, **1**
    correct [kəˈrekt] 1, **30**
    correctly [kəˈrektli] 1, **33**

the cost [kɔst] 2, **25**
 to cost [kɔst] (cost, cost) 2, **6**
  cotton ['kɔtn] 1, **7**
 to count [kaunt] (counted) 2, **21**
 a counter ['kauntə] 1, **30**
 a country ['kʌntri] (countries) 1, **32**
 a couple [kʌpl] 2, **21**
 of course [əv kɔ:s] 2, **3**
 a court [kɔ:t] 1, **20**
 a cousin ['kʌzn] 1, **12**
 to cover ['kʌvə] (covered) 2, **29**
 a cow [kau] 2, **27**
 a crash [kræʃ] (crashes) 2, **27**
  cricket ['krikit] 1, **16**
 a crowd [kraud] 2, **24**
 to cry [krai] (cried) 2, **6**
 a cup [kʌp] 1, **10**
 a cupboard ['kʌbəd] 1, **4**
 a customer ['kʌstəmə] 2, **21**
 to cut [kʌt] (cut, cut) 1, **28**

 a daffodil ['dæfədil] 2, **16**
  damn [dæm] 2, **2**
 a dance [dɑ:ns] 2, **14**
 to dance [dɑ:ns] (danced) 1, **18**
 a dancer ['dɑ:nsə] 1, **18**
  danger ['deindʒə] 2, **29**
  dangerous ['deindʒərəs] 1, **26**
  dangerously ['deindʒərəsli] 1, **29**
  dark [dɑ:k] 1, **35**
 a darling ['dɑ:liŋ] 2, **16**
 a date [deit] **1**, **32**
 a daughter ['dɔ:tə] 1, **12**
 a day [dei] 1, **15**
  dead [ded] 2, **22**
  dear [diə] 2, **21**
  December [di'sembə] 1, **31**
 to decide [di'said] (decided) 1, **34**
  deep [di:p] 2, **14**
  deliberately [di'libərətli] 2, **6**
  delighted [di'laitid] 2, **25**
 a dentist ['dentist] 2, **17**
 a deposit [di'pɔzit] 2, **25**
 a desert ['dezət] 2, **27**
 a design [di'zain] 2, **24**

 a designer [di'zainə] 2, **24**
 a desk [desk] 1, **32**
  desperately ['despərətli] 2, **19**
 a detail ['di:teil] 2, **25**
 a detective [di'tektiv] 1, **27**
 a diary ['daiəri] (diaries) 1, **15**
 a dictionary ['dikʃnri] (dictionaries) 1, **30**
 to die [dai] (died) 2, **20**
 a difference ['difrəns] 1, **33**
  different ['difrənt] 2, **2**
  difficult ['difikəlt] 1, **19**
 a difficulty ['difikəlti] (difficulties) 2, **24**
 a dinner ['dinə] 2, **20**
  dirty ['də:ti] (dirtier, dirtiest) 1, **23**
 to disappear [disə'piə] (disappeared) 2, **18**
 to discover [dis'kʌvə] (discovered) 2, **28**
 a dish [diʃ] (dishes) 2, **22**
 a distance ['distəns] 2, **28**
 a division [di'viʒn] 2, **24**
 to do [du:] (did, done) 1, **9**
 a doctor ['dɔktə] 1, **14**
 a dog [dɔg] 1, **3**
  do-it-yourself [du: it jə'self] 1, **34**
 a door [dɔ:] 1, **5**
 a doorbell ['dɔ:bel] 2, **16**
 a doorstep ['dɔ:step] 2, **22**
 a doorway ['dɔ:wei] 2, **15**
  Dover ['douvə] 2, **7**
  down¹ [daun] 1, **9**
  down² [daun] 1, **29**
  downstairs [daun'stɛəz] 2, **19**
  downwards ['daunwədz] 2, **24**
 a dozen ['dʌzn] 2, **16**
 to draw [drɔ:] (drew, drawn) 1, **36**
 a drawer [drɔ:] 1, **4**
 a dress [dres] (dresses) 2, **18**
 a drink [driŋk] 1, **20**
  drink [driŋk] 1, **21**
 to drink [driŋk] (drank, drunk) 1, **10**
 to drive [draiv] (drove, driven) 1, **22**
 to drive away [draiv ə'wei] (drove, driven) 2, **22**
 a driver ['draivə] 1, **22**
 a drop [drɔp] 2, **1**

to drop [drɔp] (dropped) 1, **11**
to dry [drai] (dried) 2, **1**
   during ['djuəriŋ] 2, **15**
to dye [dai] (dyed) 2, **23**

   each [i:tʃ] 2, **1**
an ear [iə] 1, **23**
   early ['ə:li] (earlier, earliest) 1, **17**
   easily ['i:zili] 1, **29**
the east [i:st] 2, **28**
   easy ['i:zi] (easier, easiest) 1, **17**
   easy-going ['i:zi 'gouiŋ] 2, **26**
to eat [i:t] (ate, eaten) 1, **13**
an edge [edʒ] 2, **21**
an editor ['editə] 2, **26**
an egg [eg] 1, **24**
   Egypt ['i:dʒipt] 2, **28**
   either ['aiðə] 2, **3**
   electric [i'lektrik] 1, **24**
   electrical [i'lektrikl] 2, **14**
an elephant ['elifənt] 2, **27**
   else [els] 2, **11**
an emergency [i'mə:dʒənsi] (emergencies)
   1, 13
   empty ['empti] (emptier, emptiest)
   1, 11
to empty ['empti] (emptied) 2, **5**
an encyclopaedia [ensaiklə'pi:diə] 2, **4**
an end [end] 1, **16**
an engagement [in'geidʒmənt] 2, **14**
an engine ['endʒin] 2, **3**
   England ['iŋglənd] 1, **20**
   English ['iŋgliʃ] 1, **17**
an Englishman ['iŋgliʃmən] (English-
   men) 1, **36**
   enough [i'nʌf] 2, **15**
to enter ['entə] (entered) 2, **30**
an enthusiast [in'θju:ziæst] 2, **8**
   enthusiastic [inθju:zi'æstik] 2, **10**
   enthusiastically [inθju:zi'æstikli] 2, **10**
an entrance ['entrəns] 2, **19**
an envelope ['envəloup] 1, **28**
   enviously ['enviəsli] 2, **30**
   equipment [i'kwipmənt] 1, **29**
   er [ə:] 1, **12**

an escalator ['eskəleitə] 2, **24**
   especially [i'speʃli] 2, **25**
   etc. [it'setrə] 1, **2**
   even ['i:vn] 2, **19**
an evening ['i:vniŋ] 1, **15**
   ever ['evə] 1, **24**
   every ['evri] 1, **16**
   everybody ['evribɔdi] 1, **20**
   everything ['evriθiŋ] 1, **20**
   everywhere ['evriwɛə] 1, **27**
   exact [ig'zækt] 2, **15**
   exactly [ig'zæktli] 1, **35**
an examination [igzæmin'eiʃn] 2, **2**
for example [fər ig'za:mpl] 2, **22**
   excellent ['eksələnt] 2, **22**
   except [ik'sept] 2, **17**
to excite [ik'sait] (excited) 1, **36**
   excitedly [ik'saitidli] 1, **36**
   exciting [ik'saitiŋ] 1, **36**
to exclaim [iks'kleim] (exclaimed) 2, **22**
   excuse me [iks'kju:z mi:] 1, **17**
an exercise ['eksəsaiz] 1, **17**
an exhibition [eksi'biʃn] 2, **23**
the expense [iks'pens] 2, **6**
   expensive [iks'pensiv] 1, **6**
to explain [iks'plein] (explained) 1, **27**
an expression [iks'preʃn] 2, **13**
an eye [ai] 1, **7**

   a face [feis] 1, **12**
in fact [in fækt] 2, **25**
   faint [feint] 2, **4**
to faint [feint] (fainted) 2, **4**
   faintly ['feintli] 2, **18**
   faithfully ['feiθfuli] 2, **30**
to fall [fɔ:l] (fell, fallen) 1, **27**
   a family ['fæmli] (families) 1, **12**
   famous ['feiməs] 2, **19**
   far¹ [fa:] 1, **32**
   far² [fa:] 2, **19**
   far-away ['fa:rəwei] 2, **13**
   fast¹ [fa:st] 1, **23**
   fast² [fa:st] 2, **27**
to fasten ['fa:sn] (fastened) 1, **33**
   a father ['fa:ðə] 1, **12**

a fault [fɔːlt] 1, **13**
favourite ['feivrit] 1, **15**
February ['februəri] 1, **31**
to feed [fiːd] (fed, fed) 2, **28**
to feel [fiːl] (felt, felt) 1, **36**
to feel for [fiːl fə] (felt, felt) 2, **21**
to feel like [fiːl laik] (felt, felt) 2, **9**
few [fjuː] 1, **21**
a few [fjuː] 1, **21**
a field [fiːld] 2, **29**
fierce [fiəs] 2, **29**
fiercely ['fiəsli] 2, **28**
to file [fail] (filed) 2, **19**
to fill [fil] (filled) 1, **10**
film¹ [film] 1, **11**
film² [film] 1, **18**
to film [film] (filmed) 2, **19**
finally ['fainəli] 1, **31**
to find [faind] (found, found) 1, **24**
to find out [faind aut] (found, found) 2, **9**
fine¹ [fain] 1, **35**
fine² [fain] 2, **12**
a finger ['fiŋgə] 1, **16**
to finish ['finiʃ] (finished) 1, **21**
a fire [faiə] 1, **8**
a fireplace ['faiəpleis] 2, **6**
first [fəːst] 1, **21**
at first [ət fəːst] 2, **15**
a fish [fiʃ] (fish) 1, **19**
fish [fiʃ] 1, **21**
to fish [fiʃ] (fished) 1, **27**
a fisherman ['fiʃəmən] (fishermen) 2, **22**
a flask [flaːsk] 2, **29**
a flat [flæt] 2, **6**
a floor [flɔː] 1, **5**
Florence ['flɔrəns] 1, **35**
a florist ['flɔrist] 2, **11**
flour [flauə] 1, **24**
a flower [flauə] 2, **1**
to fly [flai] (flew, flown) 1, **11**
to follow ['fɔlou] (followed) 2, **12**
food [fuːd] 1, **21**
a foot [fut] (feet) 1, **11**
a football ['futbɔːl] 1, **16**
football ['futbɔːl] 1, **16**

for [fɔː, fə] 1, **12**
forbidden [fə'bidn] 1, **17**
a forecast ['fɔːkaːst] 1, **35**
a forecaster ['fɔːkaːstə] 1, **36**
to forget [fə'get] (forgot, forgotten) 1, **27**
to forget about [fə'get ə'baut] (forgot, forgotten) 2, **15**
a fork [fɔːk] 1, **21**
formal ['fɔːml] 2, **23**
formally ['fɔːməli] 2, **25**
a fortnight ['fɔːtnait] 2, **8**
forward ['fɔːwəd] 2, **15**
France [fraːns] 1, **32**
free [friː] 1, **34**
French [frentʃ] 1, **32**
Friday ['fraidi] 1, **15**
a friend [frend] 1, **6**
friendly ['frendli] 1, **32**
from [frɔm, frəm] 1, **13**
a front [frʌnt] 2, **4**
in front of [in frʌnt əv] 1, **25**
fruit [fruːt] **1**, **21**
Fry [frai] 1, **20**
full [ful] 1, **14**
fun [fʌn] 2, **20**
funny ['fʌni] (funnier, funniest) 2, **4**
fur [fəː] 1, **7**
furniture ['fəːnitʃə] 2, **21**
further ['fəːðə] 2, **30**
the future ['fjuːtʃə] 1, **35**

gaily ['geili] 2, **28**
a game [geim] 1, **26**
a garage ['gæraːʒ] 2, **21**
a garden ['gaːdn] 1, **20**
to gasp [gaːsp] (gasped) 2, **28**
Geneva [dʒə'niːvə] 2, **24**
a gentleman ['dʒentlmən] (gentlemen) 1, **36**
gently ['dʒentli] 2, **5**
geography [dʒi'ɔgrəfi] 2, **23**
George [dʒɔːdʒ] 1, **12**
German ['dʒəːmən] 1, **32**
Germany ['dʒəːməni] 2, **24**
to get [get] (got, got) 1, **10**
to get back¹ [get bæk] (got, got) 2, **3**

to get back² [get bæk] (got, got) 2, **9**
to get (something) down [get daun]
   (got, got) 2, **3**
to get (somebody) down [get daun]
   (got, got) 2, **27**
to get home [get houm] (got, got) 2, **9**
to get married [get 'mærid] (got,
   got) 2, **13**
to get off [get ɔf] (got, got) 2, **9**
to get on [get ɔn] (got, got) 2, **15**
to get out [get aut] (got, got) 2, **9**
to get ready [get 'redi] (got, got) 2, **10**
to get rid of [get rid əv] (got, got) 2, **25**
to get up [get ʌp] (got, got) 1, **19**
to get worried [get 'wʌrid] (got, got)
   2, **24**
a girl [gə:l] 1, **1**
to give [giv] (gave, given) 1, **12**
to give away [giv ə'wei] (gave,
   given) 2, **9**
to give back [giv bæk] (gave, given) **2**, **3**
to give (somebody) a hand with [giv ə
   hænd wið] (gave, given) 2, **9**
glad [glæd] (gladder, gladdest] 1, **26**
a glass [glɑ:s] 1, **21**
glass [glɑ:s] 1, **6**
glasses ['glɑ:siz] 1, **6**
a glove [glʌv] 1, **4**
glue [glu:] 1, **12**
to go [gou] (went, gone) 1, **9**
to go away [gou ə'wei] (went, gone) 2, **9**
to go back [gou bæk] (went, gone) 2, **3**
to go by [gou bai] (went, gone) 2, **9**
to go down [gou daun] (went, gone)
   2, **14**
to go in [gou in] (went, gone) 2, **9**
to go into [gou 'intu] (went, gone) 2, **9**
to go out [gou aut] (went, gone) 2, **5**
to go round [gou raund] (went, gone)
   2, **9**
to go up [gou ʌp] (went, gone) 2, **9**
gold [gould] 2, **29**
golden ['gouldən] 2, **25**
a goldfish ['gouldfiʃ] (goldfish) 1, **26**
good [gud] (better, best) 1, **3**
goodbye [gud'bai] 1, **7**

good heavens [gud 'hevnz] 2, **29**
a grandchild ['græn'tʃaild] (grand-
   children) 1, **13**
a granddaughter ['græn'dɔ:tə] 1, **17**
a grandfather ['græn'fɑ:ðə] 1, **12**
a grandmother ['græn'mʌðə] 1, **12**
a grandparent ['græn'pɛərənt] 1, **12**
a grandson ['græn'sʌn] 1, **12**
grass [grɑ:s] 2, **2**
great [greit] 2, **12**
Great Britain [greit 'britən] 2, **28**
Greece [gri:s] 1, **36**
Greek [gri:k] 1, **36**
green [gri:n] 1, **23**
grey [grei] 1, **7**
Grey [grei] 1, **14**
ground [graund] 1, **11**
a group [gru:p] 2, **6**
to grow [grou] (grew, grown) 2, **23**
guiltily ['giltili] 2, **4**
guilty ['gilti] 2, **4**
a guitar [gi'tɑ:] 1, **15**
a gun [gʌn] 2, **28**

had better [həd 'betə] 2, **24**
hair [hɛə] 1, **23**
a hairbrush ['hɛəbrʌʃ] (hairbrushes)
   1, **34**
a hairdresser ['hɛədresə] 1, **15**
a half [hɑ:f] (halves) 1, **17**
halfway ['hɑ:lf'wei] 2, **19**
a hall [hɔ:l] 1, **4**
Hampstead ['hæmpsted] 1, **14**
a hand [hænd] 1, **6**
a handbag ['hændbæg] 1, **4**
a handkerchief ['hæŋkətʃi:f] (handker-
   chieves) 2, **14**
a handle ['hændl] 2, **23**
to hang [hæŋ] (hung, hung) 2, **23**
to happen ['hæpn] (happened) 1, **20**
happily ['hæpili] 2, **7**
happy ['hæpi] (happier, happiest)
   1, **26**
hard¹ [hɑ:d] 1, **5**
hard² [hɑ:d] 2, **5**

hard³ [hɑːd] 1, **35**
a hat [hæt] 1, **7**
to hate [heit] (hated) 2, **21**
to have [hæv] (had, had) 1, **7**
to have to [hæv tu] (had, had) 2, **16**
he [hiː] 1, **3**
a head [hed] 1, **1**
a heap [hiːp] 2, **20**
to hear [hiə] (heard, heard) 1, **33**
heavily ['hevili] 2, **7**
heavy ['hevi] (heavier, heaviest) 1, **6**
a helicopter ['helikɔptə] 1, **20**
hello [he'lou] 1, **2**
a helmet ['helmit] 1, **26**
help [help] 2, **12**
to help [help] (helped) 1, **20**
a helper ['helpə] 1, **29**
helpful ['helpfl] 2, **22**
helpfully ['helpfuli] 1, **33**
her¹ [həː, hə] 1, **3**
her² [həː, hə] 1, **12**
here [hiə] 1, **4**
hers [həːz] 1, **23**
herself [hə'self] 1, **34**
hey [hei] 1, **3**
to hide [haid] (hid, hidden) 2, **19**
high [hai] 1, **5**
him [him] 1, **12**
himself [him'self] 1, **34**
to hire [haiə] (hired) 2, **18**
hire-purchase [haiə 'pəːtʃəs] 2, **25**
his¹ [hiz] 1, **3**
his² [hiz] 1, **23**
history ['histri] 2, **23**
to hit [hit] (hit, hit) 1, **16**
hockey ['hɔki] 2, **30**
to hold [hould] (held, held) 1, **11**
to hold out [hould aut] (held, held) 2, **10**
to hold up [hould ʌp] (held, held) 2, **13**
a hole [houl] 1, **5**
a holiday ['hɔlidi] 1, **36**
a home [houm] 1, **15**
home [home] 1, **22**
home-made ['houm'meid] 1, **33**
homework ['houmwəːk] 2, **17**

a honeymoon ['hʌnimuːn] 2, **17**
to hope [houp] (hoped) 2, **11**
hopeful ['houpful] 2, **15**
horrible ['hɔribl] 1, **10**
a horse [hɔːs] 1, **1**
a hospital ['hɔspitl] 1, **14**
hot [hɔt] (hotter, hottest) 1, **16**
a hotel [hou'tel] 1, **18**
an hour [auə] 1, **26**
a house [haus] 1, **4**
how¹ [hau] 1, **5**
how² [hau] 2, **12**
how about [hau ə'baut] 2, **30**
however [hau'evə] 2, **12**
huge [hjuːdʒ] 2, **22**
a hundred ['hʌndrəd] 1, **23**
hungry ['hʌŋgri] (hungrier, hungriest) 1, **16**
a hurry ['hʌri] 2, **3**
a husband ['hʌzbənd] 1, **12**
a hut [hʌt] 1, **20**

I [ai] **1**, **3**
ice [ais] 1, **21**
an icecream ['aiskriːm] 2, **28**
icy ['aisi] 2, **30**
an idea [ai'diə] 1, **13**
if [if] 1, **34**
ill [il] 1, **15**
to imagine [i'mædʒin] (imagined) 2, **27**
immediately [i'miːdjətli] 2, **27**
impatient [im'peiʃnt] 2, **24**
impolite [impə'lait] 2, **21**
important [im'pɔːtənt] 2, **19**
impossible [im'pɔsibl] 2, **29**
in [in] 1, **4**
inexpensive [iniks'pensiv] 2, **27**
informal [in'fɔːml] 2, **23**
informally [in'fɔːməli] 2, **29**
ink [iŋk] 1, **24**
an inquiry [in'kwaiəri] 2, **25**
inside¹ [in'said] 1, **26**
inside² [in'said] 1, **28**
inside³ [in'said] 2, **18**
instead of [in'sted əv] 2, **9**

to lend [lend] (lent, lent) 1, **14**
  less¹ [les] 2, **7**
  less² [les] 2, **7**
  less³ [les] 2, **22**
a lesson ['lesn] 2, **13**
to let [let] (let, let) 2, **8**
to let go [let gou] (let, let) 2, **18**
to let in [let in] (let, let) 2, **16**
  let's [lets] 2, **8**
a letter ['letə] 1, **32**
a librarian [lai'brɛəriən] 2, **1**
a library ['laibrəri] (libraries) 1, **30**
to lick [lik] (licked) 2, **28**
to lie [lai] (lay, lain) 1, **14**
to lie down [lai daun] (lay, lain) 1, **14**
a life [laif] (lives) 2, **15**
a lift [lift] 1, **13**
a light [lait] 2, **14**
  light¹ [lait] 1, **18**
  light² [lait] 1, **35**
  like [laik] 1, **23**
to like [laik] (liked) 1, **32**
a line [lain] 1, **16**
a lion [laiən] 2, **26**
a lipstick ['lipstik] 2, **2**
  Lisbon ['lizbən] 1, **35**
a list [list] 1, **17**
to listen ['lisn] (listened) 1, **10**
to listen to ['lisn tu] (listened) 1, **13**
  little¹ ['litl] 1, **5**
  little² ['litl] 1, **21**
  little³ ['litl] 1, **34**
a little ['litl] 1, **21**
to live [liv] (lived) 1, **17**
a living-room ['liviŋ rum] 1, **17**
  Liz [liz] 1, **3**
  Ljubljana ['ljub'ljɑ:nə] 1, **17**
  local ['loukl] 2, **17**
  London ['lʌndən] 1, **17**
  long¹ [lɔŋ] 1, **21**
  long² [lɔŋ] 1, **24**
  long-playing ['lɔŋ'pleiiŋ] 2, **6**
a look [luk] 2, **16**
to look¹ [luk] (looked) 1, **9**
to look² [luk] (looked) 2, **6**
to look after [luk 'ɑ:ftə] (looked) 2, **3**

to look at [luk ət] (looked) 1, **9**
to look back [luk bæk] (looked) 2, **2**
to look down [luk daun] (looked) 2, **9**
to look for [luk fə] (looked) 1, **13**
to look forward to [luk 'fɔ:wəd tu]
    (looked) 2, **14**
to look round [luk raund] (looked) 2, **9**
to look through [luk θru:] (looked) 2, **6**
to look up [luk ʌp] (looked) 2, **4**
to lose [lu:z] (lost, lost) 1, **23**
  lost [lɔst] 2, **12**
  lot [lɔt] 1, **17**
a lot [lɔt] 1, **19**
a lot of [lɔt əv] 1, **12**
  loud [laud] 2, **6**
  loudly ['laudli] 2, **6**
  love [lʌv] 1, **14**
to love [lʌv] (loved) 2, **2**
a lover ['lʌvə] 2, **8**
  low [lou] 1, **18**
  lucky ['lʌki] (luckier, luckiest) 2, **12**
a lunch [lʌntʃ] (lunches) 1, **17**
  Luton ['lu:tn] 2, **29**

a machine [mə'ʃi:n] 1, **10**
  mad [mæd] 2, **8**
  madam ['mædəm] 2, **2**
  Madrid [mə'drid] 1, **35**
a magazine [mægə'zi:n] 2, **26**
  magic ['mædʒik] 1, **28**
a magician [mə'dʒiʃn] 1, **28**
to make [meik] (made, made) 1, **12**
to make up [meik ʌp] (made, made)
    2, **10**
  male [meil] 2, **28**
  Malta ['mɔltə] 1, **35**
a man [mæn] (men) 1, **1**
a manager ['mænidʒə] 1, **20**
  Manchester ['mæntʃəstə] 2, **12**
  many¹ ['meni] 1, **5**
  many² ['meni] 1, **21**
  March [mɑ:tʃ] 1, **31**
to march [mɑ:tʃ] (marched) 2, **26**
  Margaret ['mɑ:grit] 1, **13**
a marriage ['mæridʒ] 2, **26**

Nicosia [nikə'siə] 1, **35**
a night [nait] 1, **17**
no¹ [nou] 1, **1**
no² [nou] 1, **20**
nobody ['noubədi] 1, **20**
noise [nɔiz] 2, **1**
noisily ['nɔizili] 2, **4**
noisy ['nɔizi] (noisier, noisiest) 1, **22**
none [nʌn] 1, **33**
nonsense ['nɔnsəns] 2, **26**
no one ['nou wʌn] 2, **30**
nor [nɔ:] 2, **4**
the north [nɔ:θ] 2, **28**
a nose [nouz] 1, **23**
not [nɔt] 1, **3**
a note [nout] 1, **28**
a notebook ['noutbuk] 2, **13**
nothing ['nʌθiŋ] 1, **20**
a notice ['noutis] 1, **10**
notice ['noutis] 2, **19**
to notice ['noutis] (noticed) 2, **13**
November [no'vembə] 1, **31**
now [nau] 1, **5**
nowhere ['nouwɛə] 1, **20**
a nuisance ['nju:səns] 1, **19**
a number ['nʌmbə] 1, **14**
a nurse [nə:s] 1, **14**

an objection [əb'dʒekʃən] 2, **29**
obviously ['ɔbviəsli] 2, **20**
an occasion [ə'keiʒn] 2, **25**
o'clock [ə'klɔk] 1, **16**
October [ɔk'toubə] 1, **31**
of [ɔv, əv] 1, **7**
off¹ [ɔf] 1, **18**
off² [ɔf] 1, **27**
an office ['ɔfis] 1, **32**
often ['ɔftn] 1, **16**
oh [ou] 1, **1**
oh dear [ou diə] 1, **20**
oil [ɔil] 2, **14**
old [ould] 1, **3**
on¹ [ɔn] 1, **4**
on² [ɔn] 2, **4**
once [wʌns] 1, **29**
at once [ət wʌns] 2, **17**

one [wʌn] 1, **22**
only¹ ['ounli] 1, **10**
only² ['ounli] 2, **22**
onto ['ɔntu] 2, **1**
open ['oupən] 1, **9**
to open ['oupən] (opened) 1, **10**
an opener ['oupnə] 2, **29**
an opening ['oupniŋ] 1, **13**
opposite ['ɔpəsit] 2, **26**
or [ɔ:] 1, **4**
an orange ['ɔrindʒ] 2, **18**
order ['ɔ:də] 1, **28**
to order ['ɔ:də] (ordered) 2, **30**
other¹ ['ʌðə] 1, **23**
other² ['ʌðə] 1, **35**
ought [ɔ:t] 2, **14**
our [auə] 1, **3**
ours [auəz] 1, **23**
ourselves [auə'selvz] 1, **34**
out [aut] 1, **15**
out of [aut əv] 1, **14**
outside¹ [aut'said] 1, **21**
outside² [aut'said] 1, **23**
an oven ['ʌvn] 1, **24**
over¹ ['ouvə] 1, **35**
over² ['ouvə] 2, **29**
own [oun] 2, **7**

to pack [pæk] (packed) 1, **19**
a packet ['pækit] 2, **5**
a page [peidʒ] 1, **12**
paint [pɔint] 1, **34**
to paint [peint] (painted) 1, **34**
a painter ['peintə] 1, **34**
a pair [pɛə] 1, **5**
paper ['peipə] 1, **21**
a parcel ['pɑ:sl] 2, **22**
a parent ['pɛərənt] 1, **12**
Paris ['pæris] 1, **17**
a park [pɑ:k] 1, **20**
to park [pɑ:k] (parked) 1, **21**
a part [pɑ:t] 2, **4**
particular [pə'tikjulə] 2, **14**
particularly [pə'tikjuləli] 2, **10**
a party ['pɑ:ti] (parties) 1, **15**
to pass¹ [pɑ:s] (passed) 2, **3**

to pass² [pɑ:s] (passed) 2, **11**
to pass³ [pɑ:s] (passed) 2, **23**
to pass by [pɑ:s bai] (passed) 2, **28**
a passenger ['pæsindʒə] 1, **17**
a passport ['pɑ:spɔ:t] 2, **18**
past [pɑ:st] 1, **17**
a patient ['peiʃnt] 2, **19**
patient ['peiʃnt] 2, **15**
patiently ['peiʃntli] 2, **17**
Patsy ['pætsi] 1, **23**
a pause [pɔ:z] 2, **30**
to pay [pei] (paid, paid) 1, **20**
to pay for [pei fə] (paid, paid) 2, **2**
a paydesk ['pei desk] 2, **23**
a payment ['peimənt] 2, **25**
a pedestrian [pə'destriən] 2, **28**
a pen [pen] 1, **14**
a penalty ['penəlti] (penalties) 1, **17**
a pencil ['pensil] 1, **14**
a penny ['peni] (pennies) 2, **21**
pence [pens] 1, **10**
people ['pi:pl] 1, **17**
perhaps [pə'hæps] 1, **4**
a person ['pə:sn] 1, **23**
to persuade [pəs'weid] (persuaded) 2, **22**
Peter ['pi:tə] 1, **3**
petrol ['petrəl] 1, **20**
Philippa ['filipə] 2, **6**
a 'phone [foun] 1, **36**
to 'phone [foun] ('phoned) 1, **31**
a photo ['foutou] 2, **13**
a photograph ['foutəgrɑ:f] 1, **11**
a photographer [fə'tɔgrəfə] 1, **11**
a piano [pi'ænou] 1, **33**
to pick up [pik ʌp] (picked up) 2, **2**
a picnic ['piknik] 2, **29**
a picture ['piktʃə] 1, **1**
a piece [pi:s] 1, **28**
a pile [pail] 2, **6**
a pilot ['pailət] 1, **20**
a pin [pin] 1, **16**
a pipe [paip] 2, **1**
pity ['piti] 1, **18**
a place [pleis] 2, **1**
a plan [plæn] 2, **17**

to plan [plæn] (planned) 2, **21**
a plane [plein] 1, **17**
plastic ['plæstik] 1, **6**
a plate [pleit] 1, **21**
a platform ['plætfɔ:m] 2, **24**
to play [plei] (played) 1, **16**
to play about with [plei ə'baut wið] (played) 2, **12**
a player [pleiə] 1, **16**
pleasant ['pleznt] 2, **27**
please [pli:z] 1, **7**
pleased [pli:zd] 2, **15**
a plug [plʌg] 2, **1**
a pocket ['pɔkit] 1, **30**
to point [pɔint] (pointed) 2, **3**
to point to [pɔint tu] (pointed) 2, **10**
poison ['pɔizn] 1, **12**
the police [pə'li:s] 1, **9**
a policeman [pə'li:smən] (policemen) 1, **8**
polite [pə'lait] 2, **21**
politely [pə'laitli] 2, **19**
a politician [pɔli'tiʃn] 2, **19**
a pool [pu:l] 1, **15**
poor [puə] 2, **21**
pop [pɔp] 2, **6**
Portugal ['pɔ:tjugəl] 2, **28**
possible ['pɔsibl] 2, **16**
possibly ['pɔsibli] 2, **17**
a post [poust] 1, **30**
to post [poust] (posted) 2, **12**
a postman ['poustmən] (postmen) 1, **34**
a pound [paund] 1, **17**
powder ['paudə] 2, **5**
a practice ['præktis] 2, **1**
to practise ['præktis] (practised) 1, **11**
a present ['preznt] 1, **12**
present ['preznt] 2, **25**
to press [pres] (pressed) 2, **27**
to pretend [pri'tend] (pretended) 2, **13**
prettily ['pritili] 1, **29**
pretty ['priti] (prettier, prettiest) 1, **12**
a price [prais] 2, **14**
private ['praivət] 2, **29**
a prize [praiz] 2, **10**
a programme ['prougræm] 2, **6**

room [rum] 2, **21**
a rope [roup] 2, **5**
a rose [rouz] 2, **2**
Rotterdam [rɔtə'dæm] 2, **15**
round¹ [raund] 1, **29**
round² [raund] 1, **33**
round³ [raund] 2, **29**
to rub [rʌb] (rubbed) 2, **22**
to run [rʌn] (ran, run) 1, **9**
a runner ['rʌnə] 1, **18**
to rush [rʌʃ] (rushed) 2, **16**
Russia ['rʌʃə] 2, **28**

sad [sæd] (sadder, saddest) 1, **29**
sadly ['sædli] 1, **28**
safe [seif] 1, **5**
safely ['seifli] 2, **1**
a saint [seint] 2, **2**
for sale [fə seil] 2, **21**
a salesman ['seilzmən] (salesmen) 2, **4**
a salmon ['sæmən] 2, **22**
salt [sɔlt] 1, **21**
same [seim] 1, **31**
a sandwich ['sænwitʃ] (sandwiches)
1, **21**
Sandy ['sændi] 1, **3**
Saturday ['sætədi] 1, **15**
a saucer ['sɔ:sə] 2, **6**
to save [seiv] (saved) 2, **24**
to save up [seiv ʌp] (saved) 2, **21**
to say [sei] (said, said) 1, **13**
a scarf [skɑ:f] (scarves) 1, **35**
a school [sku:l] 1, **26**
science [saiəns] 2, **23**
scissors ['sizəz] 1, **5**
a scooter ['sku:tə] 1, **2**
the sea [si:] 1, **36**
a seat [si:t] 1, **4**
a seatbelt ['si:tbelt] 2, **28**
secondhand ['sekənd'hænd] 1, **31**
a secret ['si:krət] 2, **17**
a secretary ['sekrətri] (secretaries) 1, **32**
secretly ['si:krətli] 2, **20**
to see [si:] (saw, seen) 1, **25**
to seem [si:m] (seemed) 2, **28**

selfish ['selfiʃ] 2, **26**
to sell [sel] (sold, sold) 1, **22**
to send [send] (sent, sent) 1, **16**
sensible ['sensibl] 1, **23**
a sentence ['sentəns] 1, **17**
sentimental [senti'mentl] 2, **13**
September [səp'tembə] 1, **31**
seriously ['siəriəsli] 2, **14**
service ['sə:vis] 2, **17**
a set [set] 2, **25**
a settee [se'ti:] 2, **26**
several ['sevrəl] 2, **20**
a sewing machine ['souiŋ mə'ʃi:n] 2, **11**
to shake [ʃeik] (shook, shaken) 1, **35**
shall [ʃæl] 1, **35**
a shampoo [ʃæm'pu:] 2, **10**
to share [ʃɛə] (shared) 2, **6**
she [ʃi:] 1, **3**
a sheet [ʃi:t] 2, **29**
a shelf [ʃelf] (shelves) 1, **5**
to shine [ʃain] (shone, shone) 2, **2**
a ship [ʃip] 2, **14**
a shirt [ʃə:t] 1, **3**
a shoe [ʃu:] 1, **3**
a shoelace ['ʃu:leis] 1, **20**
a shop [ʃɔp] 1, **5**
to shop [ʃɔp] (shopped) 1, **15**
short [ʃɔ:t] 1, **23**
shorthand ['ʃɔ:thænd] 1, **32**
should [ʃud] 2, **16**
a shoulder ['ʃouldə] 2, **4**
to shout [ʃaut] (shouted) 1, **23**
show [ʃou] 2, **21**
to show [ʃou] (showed, shown) 1, **14**
a shower¹ [ʃauə] 2, **1**
a shower² [ʃauə] 2, **7**
to shut [ʃʌt] (shut, shut) 1, **10**
to shut up [ʃʌt ʌp] (shut, shut) 2, **29**
a shuttlecock ['ʃʌtlkɔk] 2, **30**
a side [said] 1, **31**
side by side [said bai said] 1, **35**
Sidney ['sidni] 2, **12**
a sigh [sai] 2, **19**
to sigh [sai] (sighed) 2, **15**
silent ['sailənt] 2, **14**
silently ['sailəntli] 2, **18**

silly ['sili] (sillier, silliest) 1, **4**
silver ['silvə] 2, **25**
simple ['simpl] 2, **26**
since¹ [sins] 1, **31**
since² [sins] 2, **7**
to sing [siŋ] (sang, sung) 2, **19**
Singapore [siŋgə'pɔ:] 2, **14**
a singer ['siŋə] 2, **19**
sir [sə:] 2, **2**
a sister ['sistə] 1, **12**
to sit [sit] (sat, sat) 1, **9**
to sit at [sit ət] (sat, sat) 2, **11**
to sit down [sit daun] (sat, sat) 1, **25**
a sixpence ['sikspəns] 1, **10**
a size [saiz] 1, **18**
a ski [ski:] 2, **20**
to ski [ski:] (skied) 2, **20**
a skirt [skə:t] 1, **3**
the sky [skai] (skies) 1, **1**
Slack [slæk] 1, **32**
slacks [slæks] 1, **3**
sleep [sli:p] 2, **11**
to sleep [sli:p] (slept, slept) 1, **32**
to slide [slaid] (slid, slid) 2, **24**
a slope [sloup] 2, **20**
slow [slou] 1, **22**
slowly ['slouli] 1, **28**
small [smɔ:l] 1, **22**
smart [smɑ:t] 1, **5**
smartly ['smɑ:tli] 2, **14**
a smile [smail] 2, **18**
to smile [smail] (smiled) 2, **4**
Smith [smiθ] 1, **3**
to smoke [smouk] (smoked) 2, **1**
a smoker ['smoukə] 2, **4**
a snake [sneik] 2, **29**
snow [snou] 2, **20**
to snow [snou] (snowed) 1, **35**
so¹ [sou] 1, **18**
so² [sou] 2, **4**
so³ [sou] 2, **10**
so that [sou ðət] 2, **1**
soap [soup] 1, **26**
a sock [sɔk] 1, **3**
Sofia ['soufiə] 1, **17**
soft [sɔft] 1, **18**

softly ['sɔftli] 2, **13**
some [sʌm] 1, **7**
somebody ['sʌmbədi] 1, **20**
somehow ['sʌmhau] 2, **19**
someone ['sʌmwʌn] 2, **30**
something ['sʌmθiŋ] 1, **20**
sometimes ['sʌmtaimz] 1, **16**
somewhere ['sʌmwɛə] 1, **20**
a son [sʌn] 1, **12**
soon [su:n] 2, **3**
sorry ['sɔri] 1, **4**
the south [sauθ] 2, **28**
a spaceman ['speismæn] (spacemen) 1, **26**
Spain [spein] 2, **28**
Spanish ['spæniʃ] 1, **32**
to speak [spi:k] (spoke, spoken) 1, **20**
to speak to [spi:k tu] (spoke, spoken) 2, **1**
a speaker ['spi:kə] 1, **29**
special ['speʃl] 1, **16**
speechless ['spi:tʃləs] 2, **25**
speed [spi:d] 1, **29**
to spend [spend] (spent, spent) 1, **31**
a spider ['spaidə] 1, **7**
to spoil [spɔil] (spoilt, spoilt) 2, **22**
a spoon [spu:n] 1, **21**
a spoonful ['spu:nful] 2, **7**
a sport [spɔ:t] 1, **16**
a spring [spriŋ] 2, **6**
square [skwɛə] 2, **14**
squash [skwɔʃ] 2, **30**
a stair [stɛə] 1, **4**
a stamp [stæmp] 1, **30**
to stand [stænd] (stood, stood) 1, **9**
to stand up [stænd ʌp] (stood, stood) 1, **29**
to start [stɑ:t] (started) 1, **27**
a station ['steiʃn] 1, **8**
to stay [stei] (stayed) 1, **15**
to stay up [stei ʌp] (stayed) 2, **11**
a stick [stik] 1, **28**
still¹ [stil] 1, **10**
still² [stil] 2, **20**
Stockholm ['stɔkhoum] 1, **35**
a stocking ['stɔkiŋ] 1, **3**

that¹ [ðæt] 1, **1**
that² [ðət] 1, **13**
that³ [ðət] 2, **6**
the [ðə] 1, **1**
a theatre ['θiətə] 1, **15**
their [ðɛə] 1, **10**
theirs [ðɛəz] 1, **23**
them [ðem, ðəm] 1, **12**
themselves [ðəm'selvz] 1, **34**
then [ðen] 1, **12**
there¹ [ðɛə] 1, **4**
there² [ðɛə] 1, **5**
these [ði:z] 1, **2**
they [ðei] 1, **2**
thick [θik] 2, **5**
a thief [θi:f] (thieves) 1, **3**
thin [θin] (thinner, thinnest) 2, **7**
a thing [θiŋ] 1, **18**
to think [θiŋk] (thought, thought) 1, **19**
to think about [θiŋk ə'baut] (thought, thought) 2, **2**
to think of [θiŋk əv] (thought, thought) 2, **17**
thirsty ['θə:sti] (thirstier, thirstiest) 1, **16**
this [ðis] 1, **1**
those [ðouz] 1, **2**
a thought [θɔ:t] 2, **15**
a thousand ['θauzənd] 2, **21**
through [θru:] 1, **9**
to throw [θrou] (threw, thrown) 1, **12**
to throw about [θrou ə'baut] (threw, thrown) 2, **5**
to throw away [θrou ə'wei] (threw, thrown) 1, **12**
to throw up [θrou ʌp] (threw, thrown) 2, **1**
Thursday ['θə:zdi] 1, **15**
a ticket ['tikit] 1, **15**
a tie [tai] 1, **3**
Tim [tim] 1, **13**
time [taim] 1, **16**
a time [taim] 1, **17**
a timetable ['taimteibl] 1, **34**
a tin [tin] 1, **24**
tired [taiəd] 1, **16**

a title ['taitl] 2, **11**
to [tu, tə] 1, **9**
tobacco [tə'bækou] 2, **1**
today [tə'dei] 1, **11**
together [tə'geðə] 1, **33**
together with [tə'geðə wið] 2, **10**
Tom [tɔm] 1, **3**
tomorrow [tə'mɔrou] 1, **15**
tonight [tə'nait] 1, **25**
Tony ['touni] 1, **13**
too¹ [tu:] 1, **1**
too² [tu:] 1, **18**
tooth [tu:θ] (teeth) 2, **5**
a toothbrush ['tu:θbrʌʃ] (toothbrushes) 2, **5**
toothpaste ['tu:θpeist] 2, **6**
a top [tɔp] 1, **20**
to touch [tʌtʃ] (touched) 2, **28**
towards [tə'wɔ:dz] 1, **29**
a town [taun] 2, **14**
traffic ['træfik] 2, **20**
a train [trein] 1, **6**
transistor [træn'sistə] 2, **8**
travel ['trævl] 1, **32**
to travel ['trævl] (travelled) 1, **32**
a tree [tri:] 1, **11**
a trick [trik] 2, **23**
a trolley ['trɔli] 1, **25**
trouble ['trʌbl] 1, **20**
trousers ['trauzəz] 2, **1**
true [tru:] (truer, truest) 1, **17**
truth [tru:θ] 2, **4**
to try [trai] (tried, tried) 1, **31**
a tube [tju:b] 2, **29**
Tuesday ['tju:zdi] 1, **15**
Turkey ['tə:ki] 2, **28**
a turn [tə:n] 2, **28**
to turn [tə:n] (turned) 1, **33**
to turn off [tə:n ɔf] (turned) 2, **1**
to turn on [tə:n ɔn] (turned) 2, **1**
to turn over [tə:n 'ouvə] (turned) 2, **10**
to turn round [tə:n raund] (turned) 1, **33**
to turn up [tə:n ʌp] (turned) 2, **14**
twice [twais] 2, **8**
a twin [twin] 1, **33**

to type [taip] (typed) 2, **29**
  typing ['taipiŋ] 1, **32**
  a typewriter ['taipraitə] 2, **20**
  a typist ['taipist] 2, **27**

ugly ['ʌgli] (uglier, ugliest) 1, **18**
an umbrella [ʌm'brelə] 2, **23**
  uncertainly [ʌn'sɔ:tənli] 2, **19**
an uncle ['ʌŋkl] 1, **12**
  uncomfortable [ʌn'kʌmfətəbl] 1, **22**
  uncomfortably [ʌn'kʌmfətəbli] 1, **29**
  under ['ʌndə] 1, **4**
the underground ['ʌndəgraund] 2, **24**
  underlined ['ʌndəlaind] 2, **28**
  underneath [ʌndə'ni:θ] 2, **22**
to understand [ʌndə'stænd] (under-
    stood, understood) 1, **20**
  unfriendly [ʌn'frendli] 2, **29**
  unhappily [ʌn'hæpili] 1, **25**
  unhappy [ʌn'hæpi] (unhappier,
    unhappiest) 1, **31**
  uninteresting [ʌn'intrəstiŋ] 2, **14**
a unit ['ju:nit] 1, **1**
  unkind [ʌn'kaind] 2, **15**
  unkindly [ʌn'kaindli] 2, **8**
  unless [ʌn'les] 2, **26**
  unlucky [ʌn'lʌki] (unluckier,
    unluckiest) 2, **27**
to unpack [ʌn'pæk] (unpacked) 2, **29**
  until [ʌn'til] 2, **11**
  untrue [ʌn'tru:] 1, **29**
  unusual [ʌn'ju:ʒuəl] 2, **16**
  up¹ [ʌp] 1, **9**
  up² [ʌp] 1, **29**
  upstairs [ʌp'steəz] 1, **21**
  up to [ʌp tu] 1, **16**
  upwards ['ʌpwədz] 2, **24**
  us [ʌs] 1, **13**
to use [ju:z] (used) 2, **1**
  used to [ju:s tu] 2, **23**
  usual ['ju:ʒuəl] 1, **36**
as usual [əz 'ju:ʒuəl] 2, **7**
  usually ['ju:ʒuəli] 1, **16**

Valentine ['væləntain] 2, **2**
a van [væn] 2, **28**
a vase [vɑ:z] 2, **16**
  Venice ['venis] 1, **17**
a verb [və:b] 2, **22**
  very ['veri] 1, **3**
  very well ['veri wel] 1, **12**
a vicar ['vikə] 2, **17**
  Vienna [vi'enə] 1, **32**
a violet ['vaiələt] 2, **2**
a violin [vaiə'lin] 1, **33**
a violinist [vaiə'linist] 2, **16**
a visit ['vizit] 2, **16**
to visit ['vizit] (visited) 2, **7**
a visitor ['vizitə] 2, **16**
a voice [vɔis] 1, **25**

a wage [weidʒ] 1, **34**
a waist [weist] 2, **11**
to wait [weit] (waited) 1, **12**
to wait for [weit fə] (waited) 1, **13**
a waiter ['weitə] 2, **21**
to wake up [weik ʌp] (woke, woken)
    2, **24**
a walk [wɔ:k] 2, **13**
to walk [wɔ:k] (walked) 1, **9**
to walk away [wɔ:k ə'wei] (walked) 2, **9**
to walk into [wɔ:k 'intu] (walked) 2, **10**
to walk round [wɔ:k raund] (walked)
    2, **23**
a walker ['wɔ:kə] 1, **18**
a wall [wɔ:l] 1, **13**
a wallet ['wɔlit] 1, **30**
to want [wɔnt] (wanted) 1, **17**
  warm [wɔ:m] 1, **7**
to wash [wɔʃ] (washed) 1, **24**
to wash up [wɔʃ ʌp] (washed) 1, **24**
a watch [wɔtʃ] (watches) 2, **11**
to watch [wɔtʃ] (watched) 1, **19**
a watcher ['wɔtʃə] 1, **34**
  water ['wɔ:tə] 1, **21**
to wave [weiv] (waved) 2, **24**
  wax [wæks] 2, **23**
  waxwork ['wækswə:k] 2, **23**
a way [wei] 2, **18**

by the way [bai ðə wei] 1, **35**
   we [wiː] 1, **7**
   weak [wiːk] 2, **23**
   weakly ['wiːkli] 2, **11**
  to wear [wɛə] (wore, worn) 1, **16**
   weather ['weðə] 1, **35**
   wedded ['wedid] 2, **18**
  a wedding ['wediŋ] 2, **17**
   Wednesday ['wenzdi] 1, **15**
  a week [wiːk] 1, **15**
  a weekend ['wiːkend] 2, **12**
  as well as [əz wel əz] 1, **25**
   well¹ [wel] 1, **18**
   well² [wel] 1, **31**
   well³ [wel] 2, **22**
   West [west] 1, **15**
  the west [west] 2, **28**
   wet [wet] (wetter, wettest) 1, **22**
   what¹ [wɔt] 1, **1**
   what² [wɔt] 1, **6**
   what³ [wɔt] 1, **15**
   what⁴ [wɔt] 1, **17**
   whatever [wɔ'tevə] 2, **12**
  a wheel [wiːl] 2, **11**
  ·when¹ [wen] 1, **15**
   when² [wen] 2, **8**
   whenever [we'nevə] 2, **12**
   where¹ [wɛə] 1, **4**
   where² [wɛə] 1, **34**
   where³ [wɛə] 2, **5**
   wherever [wɛə'revə] 2, **12**
   whether ['weðə] 2, **21**
   which¹ [witʃ] 1, **22**
   which² [witʃ] 1, **29**
   which³ [witʃ] 2, **8**
   while [wail] 2, **2**
   whisky ['wiski] 1, **21**
  a whisper ['wispə] 2, **21**
  to whisper ['wispə] (whispered) 2, **21**
   white [wait] 1, **4**
   who¹ [huː] 1, **3**
   who² [huː] 1, **30**
   who³ [huː] 2, **7**
   whoever [hu:'evə] 2, **12**
   whose¹ [hu:z] 2, **4**
   whose² [hu:z] 2, **4**

   why¹ [wai] 1, **9**
   why² [wai] 2, **1**
   wide [waid] 2, **11**
  a wife [waif] (wives) 1, **9**
   will [wil] 1, **35**
   Wimbledon ['wimbldən] 2, **8**
  to win [win] (won, won) 2, **14**
   wind [wind] 2, **7**
   Windermere ['windəmiə] 2, **7**
  a window ['windou] 1, **6**
   wine [wain] 1, **21**
  a wing [wiŋ] 1, **1**
  a winter ['wintə] 2, **6**
  to wish [wiʃ] (wished) 2, **30**
   with [wið] 1, **8**
   without [wiðaut] 2, **2**
  a woman ['wumən] (women) 1, **12**
  to wonder ['wʌndə] (wondered) 2, **16**
   wonderful ['wʌndəfl] 1, **32**
   wood [wud] 1, **6**
   wool [wul] 1, **7**
  a word [wəːd] 1, **21**
   work [wəːk] 1, **23**
  to work [wəːk] (worked) 1, **10**
  a worker ['wəːkə] 1, **23**
  a workman ['wəːkmən] 1, **34**
  the world [wəːld] 2, **8**
  to worry ['wʌri] (worried) 1, **26**
  to worry about ['wʌri ə'baut] (worried) 2, **6**
   would [wud] 2, **16**
  a wrist [rist] 2, **23**
  to write [rait] (wrote, written) 1, **12**
  to write down [rait daun] (wrote, written) 2, **10**
  to write out [rait aut] (wrote, written) 2, **10**
  to write to [rait tu] (wrote, written) 2, **20**
  a writer ['raitə] 1, **29**
   wrong [rɔŋ] 1, **25**

  a yard [jɑːd] 1, **23**
  a year [jiə] 1, **17**
   yellow ['jelou] 1, **23**

yes [jes] 1, **1**
yesterday ['jestədi] 1 **26**
yet [jet] 2, **7**
you [ju:, ju] 1, **3**
young [jʌŋ] 1, **12**
your [jɔ:, jə] 1, **2**
yours [jɔ:z] 1, **23**
yourself [jɔ:'self] 1, **34**
yourselves [jɔ:'selvz] 1, **34**

zing [ziŋ] 2, **13**